Authentic Sports: The 7 Pathways to Peak Performance

Bill Lefko and Daniel Baird

Second Edition

ISBN-13: 978-1726367622
ISBN-10: 1726367622

Table of Contents

Note from the Authors

In this book, we use illustrations drawn from the lives of people who are well-known athletes. We are athletes ourselves, not trained psychologists. So when we comment on their performance we are reporting what resonates with us as athletes. We do not claim that ours is the only interpretation, or even the best one, of their successes and failures. But our conclusions lead to and agree with the premise of our philosophy.

We have nothing but respect for those who reach the highest levels of their sport. By allowing us to view their performance they give us, their fans, the opportunity to draw lessons from their example. If we have erred in our conclusions, the fault is ours, not theirs.

Introduction

Authentic Sports: The Seven Pathways to Peak Performance is first of all a book about enhancing sports performance. Second, and perhaps even more important, it is about recovering an experience of inner joy while playing sports. At the deepest level, however, the book is about accessing the ultimate state of awareness — the pinnacle of human experience. Readers will experience the book on different levels, depending upon their personal state of mind and being, but nearly all will find great benefit.

At its essence, this book challenges our most deeply-rooted assumptions about sports and how they need to be played. Our culture is deeply conditioned to believe that sports must be based in conflict: me versus you - us versus them - good versus evil - dominance versus submission - strength versus weakness - and a whole host of other comparisons on the relative scale of opposites. *Authentic Sports* calls this mindset "ego centered consciousness," and it pervades not only the world of sport but virtually every other aspect of our lives. It is rooted in duality, the world of opposites and the world of the relative. On rare occasions, usually by sheer happenstance or accident, many people have experienced a very different state - a state of inner calm, quiet mind, a feeling of appreciation and gratitude or love in its truest sense. In this transcendent state, all tension created by the world of opposites melts away and the body and mind are in the deepest state of relaxation. In this pure state of "being-ness," a feeling of joy arises that has no comparison. We refer to this state as "awareness-centered" consciousness.

Our premise is that playing sports can provide an excellent means for accessing the state of awareness-centered consciousness. The very fact that the world of sports in our culture is so dominated by the ego makes it a perfect place to identify how and where the ego arises to create tension and block energy. We have discovered seven specific areas where ego-centered consciousness constrains or even blocks the normal, free flow of energy that is required to play and experience sports at the very highest personal level, regardless of skill. This gives rise to the seven pathways, seven channels, to identify and release stuck or blocked energy. Releasing tension on even one of these pathways can create a significant shift in consciousness, resulting in an elevated level of play and enhanced experience of enjoyment. Releasing tension on all seven pathways can catapult the player to an entirely different realm, not only of playing, but of being. In that realm, performance is enhanced to its very highest level. But the real prize is transcending the burdens of ego-centered consciousness to a state that is free from tension, filled with joy, passion and connectedness to everyone and everything. All of this by simply playing a game!

My Opponent – My Friend!

Make no mistake. *Authentic Sports* proposes a radical new concept to the context of what we are accustomed to in the world of sports; that the most effective and enjoyable way to play sports is not through conflict and competition (as we have come to understand that term), but rather through unity and cooperation. Many athletes already know this to be true on some level. Even the greatest and most famous have had certain times when their performance transcended normal levels of excellence. In those rare moments, they never describe the experience with ego-based terms. Instead, they employ phrases such as "effortless," "out of my mind," or "in a zone." They feel so connected with their opponent or with the process itself that they feel as though they are on a sacred, cooperative endeavor to explore the limits of their abilities. Only when their opponent provides the greatest challenge can those limits truly be explored, so in that state there is actually a wish for the opponent to be playing at his or her very best. There is no real concern about winning or losing, no concern about the crowd or the press or what someone out there might be thinking, just a pure presence with the here and now and the challenges at hand. This state is pure ecstasy, and when the game is over an athlete who has experienced it is typically filled with humility, gratitude and awe.

Even for our finest athletes, these peak experiences are very few and far between, and seem to just happen. By uncovering the energy blocks within the seven pathways caused by ego-centered consciousness, *Authentic Sports* will guide the way to deliberately access this state so that it can be experienced on a more regular basis.

The Seven Pathways

Authentic Sports will lead you through each of the seven pathways in the following order: the *will* pathway, the *belief* pathway, the *mental* pathway, the *emotional* pathway, the *relationship* pathway, the *physical* pathway and the *spiritual* pathway. The seven pathways are presented in this order for a reason. As tension is released and energy is freed up on a given pathway, the next pathway presented is the most likely place for tension to arise. For example, as tension produced by the ego is released on the *will* pathway, the next likely place for tension to show up is through *beliefs*. As the ego is neutralized on the *belief* pathway, the next likely place for tension to arise is the *mental* pathway, or the thinking mind. *Authentic Sports* progresses through each pathway until it reaches the very last domain that gives rise to tension: the *spiritual* pathway, where the ego will tend to take credit for accessing the state of awareness-centered consciousness, and where the remedy lies in humility, surrender and gratitude.

In a world that seems to be overwhelmed with the problems of conflict and separation, to the point of threatening our very survival as a species, *Authentic Sports* offers a great promise not just for athletes, but for those who want to move the world toward cooperation instead of conflict. The operation of ego-centered consciousness in sports is but a microcosm for its operation in all of life. The same consciousness that is the source of suffering and conflict in sports is also responsible for the suffering and conflict between nations and peoples. Terrorism and war have their roots in the same consciousness that operates in the "battle" between "opponents" in sporting contests.

Authentic Sports will reveal a better way, initially through the medium of sports, that can awaken people to the fact that we really are connected — that all of our suffering comes through believing in our separateness. To really understand this natural law, it must be felt. Sports are an outstanding channel for offering an opportunity for this experience. Let's discover together the power of human potential!

Chapter 1
The Nature of Peak Performance:
The Evolution of Sports

At some point in your life you have probably experienced peak performance. That experience of being completely immersed in whatever you were doing, in a state of effortlessness; as if you were watching yourself. Whether this took place while driving a car, singing, dancing, walking, having a conversation, playing a musical instrument, or playing a sport, one thing was true, these transcendent extraordinary moments were not dependent upon what you were doing. Peak performance is available in whatever you do and can occur in any moment. What then is the nature of peak performance?

To understand peak performance you need to separate and examine the relationship between peak and performance. Performance is what you can see on the outside. In sports, performance is relative to an athlete's talents, fundamentals, acquired skill set, training, and physical conditioning. Sports training which has evolved over time enhances an athlete's performance level. Through training an athlete is able to discover what his or her body is capable of doing. We feel that most coaches believe that through training an athlete will function on an optimal level and reach the peak performance state. In reality however, all the training in the world does not create the peak performance experience.

Let's now examine the transition from performance to peak performance. 'Peak" is a state of being or level of consciousness. Performance is a state of doing or action. The peak in peak performance is accessed through a state of consciousness. You can train for sports performance but you cannot train for consciousness. This is why peak performance is so elusive even for the most highly trained athletes in the world. Peak performance is a gift of the present that comes through you. You receive peak performance.

So if consciousness is the key to integrating peak with performance; what is consciousness? Authentic sports refers to consciousness as the medium through which reality is experienced. This medium integrates, responds to, and attracts experiences. The traditional or materialist view of consciousness is that it is a physical phenomenon based in chemical reactions and survival impulses in the brain. Consciousness is viewed as an effect of time and nature. The materialist views consciousness on a singular level in terms of life as consciousness and death as not consciousness. Authentic sports views consciousness as a non-physical phenomenon. Consciousness is causal, timeless, and exists on a multidimensional level. It is capable of evolving sports performance and the world to higher and higher levels.

Consciousness evolves sports by expanding what we refer to as "feel". "Feel' is a quality of consciousness that integrates the mind and body by being present. This holistic integrated state heightens sensitivity and a sense of clarity, intensifies attention, and creates a greater awareness of all movements connected to performance. Is it any wonder that many athletes when they experience peak performance describe it in terms of "I was feeling it". The quality of "feel" can be used as the reference point for peak performance. Expanded feel is what connects peak with performance. "Feel" is the foundation for mastery in sports and in life. Expanded feel transforms what might have been an ordinary performance into an extraordinary performance. If an athlete trains without expanding feel they may increase their skill level and relative performance but they will not put the peak into performance. Personal peak performance is available to any athlete at any time regardless of skill level because it is a byproduct of expanded feel. If you raise consciousness you expand feel and you elevate performance.

We suggest that there are two distinct approaches to illuminate the nature of consciousness (feel) through the nature of sports performance and we contrast them in this way:

1. Ego-centered consciousness: a habit or a conditioned level of consciousness

2. Awareness-centered consciousness: a feel-based, unconditioned level of Consciousness.

Ego-Centered Consciousness

Ego-centered consciousness is a state where consciousness is centered in the ego, or in who you think you are. It is your ego's conditioned program which spends all its time thinking, judging, analyzing and separating you from all your experiences. It constructs a mind/body separation by taking the mind out of the present moment. When the mind is outside of the present moment there is a division between the observer and the observed, the subject and the object, feel and form, and the experiencer and the experience.

Ego-centered consciousness manufactures a past identity or memory program that reacts to the world based on either desire or resistance — the *ego gratification program*. This program does not work efficiently to create peak performance because it roots the athlete into a conflicting dichotomy of either success or failure. It is based on external conditions (result oriented) which are not within the control of the athlete. The "either/or," "one-or-the-other" dichotomy divides attention and blocks both energy and feel. Its memory program conditions mental/emotional reactive patterns which tend to make sports performance, as well as life, repetitive, mundane and ordinary. A sport, as well as a life, becomes very mechanical in ego-centered consciousness and disconnected from higher states and feel.

Ego-centered consciousness avoids the present because the present contains no memory of its identity. It operates through force of habit, producing a kind of inertia which does not allow the player to adapt to the ebb and flow required for peak sports performance. Sports performance cannot be expanded through past programming. Since the present will never be exactly like the past, and the future contains countless possibilities beyond the control of the ego, peak sports performance cannot be controlled through habit, memory and thinking.

Ego-centered consciousness is locked and stuck in past experiences. It projects its conditioning into the future. It becomes inevitable that athletes will make the same mistakes over and over again. The mind remains a creature of habit, not being aware of the consciousness and the feeling state within.

Ego-centered consciousness conditions a duality of opposing

opposites — win or lose, good or bad, right or wrong — indoctrinating a constant tension and uneasiness to sports performance and to life. The athlete operates in a state of struggle, constantly in resistance to what is, and sees no other alternative. This duality of opposing forces divides attention, reducing the *feel* state necessary for peak performance.

Ego centered consciousness experiences sports performance through a domain of limited perceptions which are rooted in survival instincts, security, pleasure, pain, memory, thinking, reacting, and duality. When sports performance is perceived through these lower or conditioned levels of consciousness, peak performance is not possible. Peak performance and ego-centered consciousness are mutually exclusive.

Awareness-Centered Consciousness

Awareness-centered consciousness is your authentic state — who you really are. It is a state in which mind and body is unified in the present moment. It is our natural observing and feeling state and shows up when we begin to notice our thoughts and not treat our thinking and beliefs as who we are. It says, in effect: "I have thoughts but I am not my thoughts."

Awareness-centered consciousness recognizes and accepts all forms including the ego (programmed thought form) but views them as something manufactured by the conditioned mind. When we are in this natural feeling state we connect to the power of source energy and an integrated intelligence beyond anything known by the mind. By being in the present, awareness-centered consciousness removes the ego, bypassing the conditioned, mental and emotional reactive patterns. This transforms life and sports performance into an extraordinary, creative, original and authentic experience.

Awareness-centered consciousness is a vehicle for the evolution of sports performance. It is flexible and adapts to the continuous changes experienced in sports. It responds to experience on a moment-to-moment basis, creating unlimited potential and possibility. It creates in the present moment, which takes into account both the unknown and the known, feel and form. The unknown moving through the known, or *feel* moving through *form*, is the basis of peak performance. Peak performance is a creative "feel" state, which cannot be programmed.

Awareness-centered consciousness perceives experience through the higher levels of consciousness such as intuition, spontaneity, origination, creativity, observation and deliberateness. When sports performance is connected to higher levels of consciousness, peak performance is a natural outcome.

Awareness-Centered Consciousness vs. Ego-Centered Consciousness

When do you know that you are accessing *awareness-centered consciousness* rather than *ego-centered consciousness*? The ultimate answer is — you will feel it. Here are some reference points that will identify the state of consciousness you are experiencing.

The following are a few of the attributes of Ego-Centered Consciousness:

Tension
Over excitement
Apathy

Strong desire to win (ambition)
Lack of desire
Exhaustion
Struggle and conflict
Emotional Highs and lows
Trying too hard
Need for approval
Self-judgment
Blaming
The need to be right
Over control
Excessive effort

The list could go on and on, because the egotistical world of desire/resist can manifest in innumerable states. The common denominator in all of these states is a separation between what *is* and what the ego *would like*, or between what *is* and what the ego fears *will not be*. These separations create tension that blocks energy "feel" from flowing freely. There is a sense of clenching — trying to grab onto something — to *make* something happen rather than *allowing* it to happen.

In contrast, here are some of the attributes of Awareness-Centered Consciousness:

Inspiration from within
Freedom
Creativity
Spontaneity
Joy
Love
Effortlessness
Ease

Boundless energy
Intuition
Allowing

When you are in a state of awareness-centered consciousness you are still playing the game for all it is worth, but you are playing for different reasons. You play for the pure enjoyment of the challenge of mastering the game's objectives. Ironically, when the ego no longer has strong attachments to the outcome of a game due to external reasons, performance, by external standards, greatly improves. You will find that the real reward is simply being in the state that you are in, regardless of outcome, which transcends the normal struggle state of ego-centered consciousness.

When any action is performed through awareness-centered consciousness, peak performance has occurred in that moment. When these sports-relevant actions and moments flow together continuously you enter the state of peak performance commonly referred to as "the zone." When an athlete's actions are distracted or interrupted, blocking the natural energy feel and flow, the ego performer has taken over.

The Ego Performer

The ego sports performer experiences sports through ego-centered consciousness which operates on the reactive, survival level of consciousness. The ego performer emulates the classic case of Pavlov's dog, constantly reacting to its conditioning. For the ego sports performer, the *thinking* program oscillates between the past and the future denying the present moment where *feel* exists.

The ego sports performer discounts consciousness and feel as causal and wants to reverse-engineer the cause and effect. He treats the athletic form or the effects of what is *seen* as the *cause* of sports performance. What *Authentic Sports* performance refers to as reverse-engineering is the ego performer's way of working backwards from the result. What this means is that the ego sports performer tries to replicate a desired outcome. He sees a great sports performance that has taken place naturally through higher consciousness and feel, and then tries to copy or duplicate it mechanically. The ego performer wants to possess, control and own the sports performance so he can continue to clone peak performance in the future. *Authentic Sports* performance refers to this as the "Catch-22" of the ego. Catch-22, based on the 1970 movie of the same name, is defined as a situation in which a desired outcome or solution is impossible to attain because of a set of inherently illogical rules or conditions. The Catch-22 of reverse engineering is that the ego sports performer can never control the present through the past.

The ego sports performer believes that he can, through reverse engineering, divorce consciousness and feel from the performance. He believes that by desiring or attaching its image to positive qualities such as positive thinking, body language, and concentration, and then resisting the negative qualities such as apathy, unfocused attention and negative body language, he can make performance mechanical.

Tricks of the Ego Sports Performer

When you notice what your ego is trying to achieve out of a sporting activity in which you are engaged, your first temptation will probably be to judge and resist it. This is actually a trick of the ego. The ego wants to say, "OK, now I've got it! The duality of the ego is painful and getting in the way of my performance so I need to get rid of the ego." But this is bringing the very same mindset of the ego right back into play. The ego is still trying to replicate an outcome.

Most of us, living in the concerns of the ego, do not want to see our own self-serving ego at work. The ego deludes us into believing that it is a separate self. There is tremendous relief in just acknowledging that we are almost always operating in the concerns of the ego. This is just the way it is. Trying to judge or condemn the fact won't change it. In fact, it is a well-known principle of psychology as well as physics that resisting something actually provides it with energy to stay in place. It follows the law of attention. What you pay attention to grows. Therefore what you resist persists.

The ego is trapped in the domain of ego-centered consciousness. Like a coin that consists of both heads and tails, the ego does not realize that whatever side of the ego coin shows up, it is still the same coin. One side of the coin reads inferior, the other side reads superior. The ego constantly flips the coin — one side being desire, superior, domination and strength, and the other side being resistance, inferior, submission and weakness. This will always create a mixed performance and mixed results. Peak performance cannot be manufactured. Sports' training without observation does not create a natural and timeless peak performance state. As long as the athlete is in the domain of ego-centered consciousness, peak performance is not possible.

The Authentic Sports Performer

The *Authentic Sports* performer experiences sports through the higher realms of consciousness and expanded feel. She perceives the world as existing in a neutral state, bypassing the duality of the desire/resist program. This neutral state is what we call the *observer state of consciousness* — a state in which the observer is the observed. It is a non-judgmental, ego-less state that is only available when the mind and body are unified in the present.

Observation through awareness-centered consciousness removes ego (resistance, judgment and tension), thereby unblocking energy, expanding *feel* and allowing it to flow freely towards peak performance. Observation unifies experiences by releasing tension that is a byproduct of mind and body separation. This mind/body sync joins the performance with the performer and unifies *feel* and *form,* allowing for undivided attention.

Observation connects the authentic sports performer with their natural *feel* state. It allows the athlete to be immersed in the creative process, "the power of now," to use a phrase coined by Eckart Tolle. The authentic performer taps into the creative process and draws from the unlimited potentiality of every moment, realizing that when you create from higher realms of consciousness, such as observation, intuition, spontaneity and surrendered action (action based on non-resistance) peak performance will be a natural byproduct. Peak performance is inherent to and is part of the creative process. It cannot be reverse-engineered.

The *Authentic Sports* performer, perceiving through awareness-centered consciousness, creates a holistic experience, a unification of mind, body, and spirit. This higher conscious state maximizes opportunities in every moment. Sports' training that takes place within awareness-centered consciousness moves the authentic performer towards their highest potential and peak performance.

The Seven Pathways (Dimensions) of Human Experience

Authentic Sports suggests that there are seven dimensions — energy pathways or *feel* channels for performance within the realm of human experience. The energy or feel required to enter the state of peak performance is blocked at the lower levels of consciousness and released at the higher levels of consciousness.

These pathways of sports performance act as reference points to illuminate the experiences of either the higher or lower levels of consciousness. The pathways within the realm of human experience are *Will, Belief, Mental, Emotional, Relationship, Physical, and Spiritual.*

When these pathways are accessed by the lower levels of consciousness it leads to random results, conflict and struggle. In lower-level, ego-centered consciousness the ego performer is unable to break out of the dualistic mind set or the desire to reverse engineer the natural creative process. When experienced through the ego performer, there is a manufactured set of conflicting opposites, one to be desired and one to be resisted. These conflicting opposites are:

1. *Will* Pathway - I will do it or I won't do it.
2. *Belief* Pathway - I can do it or I can't do it.
3. *Mental* Pathway - Attachment to "good" or repel what is "bad"
4. *Emotional* Pathway - Positive (love) or negative (hate) emotion.
5. *Relationship* Pathway - For (me, team) or against (you, other team).
6. *Physical* Pathway - Strong or weak
7. *Spiritual* Pathway - Pride or humiliation.

Make no mistake; *Authentic Sports* performance claims that when you are in ego-centered consciousness, you cannot experience the high end of the ego without experiencing the low end as well.

In the higher levels of consciousness, or in a unified, integrated, holistic *feel* state, the *Authentic Sports* performer connects to the creative process and peak performance. The nature of higher consciousness itself is responsible for peak performance. Higher consciousness transcends and neutralizes duality, thereby releasing energy and expanding *feel*, while eliminating any conflict or resistance blocking the peak performance state.

1. *Will* Pathway - connects to intrinsic motivation and experiences inspiration.
2. *Belief* Pathway - connects to faith and experiences the realm of all possibilities.
3. *Mental* Pathway - connects to a neutral and unattached mind and experiences freedom from judgment.
4. *Emotional* Pathway - connects to love and appreciation and experiences joy.
5. *Relationship* Pathway - connects to an integrated holistic state and experiences unity or oneness.
6. *Physical* Pathway - connects to surrendered action and body wisdom and experiences peak performance, the feeling of effortless effort.
7. *Spiritual* Pathway - connects to humility and experiences an enlightened state.

The seven pathways, within the realm of human experience, exist in a unified state when perceived though awareness-centered consciousness. However, they present a unique challenge in ego-centered consciousness where the energy and feel is blocked. Starting with the *Will* pathway, *Authentic Sports* performance will guide you in the direction of awareness-centered consciousness. It will demonstrate that within every pathway or energy/feel channel, ego centered consciousness blocks energy or *feel* and sabotages peak performance. It is time for your sports performance to be motivated by your authentic will and for you to experience the power of inspiration!

Chapter 2
Will: Pathway to Inspiration

Everything starts with the will — the seat of motivation. It is what initiates any action or activity including playing sports. *Authentic Sports* refers to the *will* as the ability of an athlete to initiate and sustain an intention. Intention shapes action in the world of sports. How an athlete initiates and sustains an intention determines the quality of her actions. Intention is molded by the level of consciousness of the individual. When an individual's will is connected to higher levels of consciousness there is unlimited energy and a natural intention to grow and to evolve.

John Wooden

Authentic Sports refers to intentions that are based in the energy to grow, as *core* intentions. Core intentions evolve while working towards the betterment of the whole, such as the team, society, or family. The legendary UCLA basketball coach John Wooden's coaching philosophy was centered on core intentions. He developed what he called the "pyramid of success," which was based on developing the character of an individual and his service to others as a pathway to the highest level of performance. This foundation allowed Wooden to win 10 NCAA basketball national championships even though it took 16 years, from 1948 when he first became head coach, until 1964 before he won his first title. In today's society, where the prevailing sentiment seems to be "win now or you're fired," this legendary coach may not have been given a chance for his philosophy to take hold and thus obtain his storied resume of success. His core intention of becoming a better person, thereby being of greater service to himself and others, is a testament to the power of higher levels of consciousness.

Wooden defined success as "peace of mind that is a direct result of self-satisfaction in knowing you did the best to become the best you are capable of becoming." Another example of a core intention based in a higher level of consciousness is, "I maximize my potential while moving towards the mastery of the game." Many great athletes who have reached the highest levels of their sport have probably been driven by a core intention that originated from a higher level of consciousness.

On the lower levels of consciousness, intention is based in divisiveness, self-centeredness, and "going against." It's result-oriented and centered in personal success. The great football genius, Vince Lombardi, is famously quoted as saying "winning isn't everything; it's the only thing." Although he later regretted saying it, this is clearly an example of an ego-based intention. Expressions such as "winners never quit and quitters never win," or "second place is just the first loser," derive their impetus from the ego.

Ego-Centered Consciousness on the Will Pathway

The *will* can derive its energy or motivation from either ego-centered consciousness or awareness-centered consciousness. When the will derives its energy or motivation from ego-centered consciousness it becomes divided, programmed, and conditioned. This happens through the opinions of others such as: coaches, parents, teachers, peers, and teammates. This indoctrination can disconnect the will's motivations from consciousness, the unknown, inspiration, personnel feel, and the present. Since consciousness is an unlimited source of creative energy, the will's motivation, which is the channel for that creative energy, is blocked in ego-centered consciousness. The will's motivation becomes based in the past (memory) and habits of thought. Consciousness and creative energy originate from the unknown and the unconditioned. Without consciousness (the unknown) flowing into form and action (the known), the will's motivation becomes mechanical or uninspired rather than authentic, creative, and inspired.

Awareness-Centered Consciousness on the Will Pathway

The will, deriving its motivation through awareness-centered consciousness, is inspired, creative and free. It is connected to the unknown, consciousness (the cause), personal feel, and the present. In awareness-centered consciousness, the will channels unlimited source energy, creative energy, and personal feel to the task at hand. It is free from past conditioning, total reliance on the known, and force of habit. When the will channels energy from the unknown or creative process, energy and feel flows into form and action continuously, on a moment to moment basis.

Intrinsic versus Extrinsic Motivation

What motivates the will to action has a profound effect, not only on sports performance but on the enjoyment of the game as well. The will can either be motivated extrinsically or intrinsically. Extrinsic motivators are factors outside of one's inner being and are rooted in the desire resistance cycle or ego-centered consciousness. They are conditioned and dualistic, operating in the domain of opposing opposites. Here there are relative winners and losers. In other words, some egos prevail over other egos out of shear willpower or strength. How many times have you heard a sports commentator say something to this effect: "This team (or this player) just wanted it more!"? And that may have been true. In the domain of ego-centered consciousness, the player or team with a greater will to win usually will prevail. But here is the question that is seldom asked. "Could that winning player or team have played at an even higher level?" *Authentic Sports'* answer is, unequivocally, "yes!" Ironically, that higher level is accessed by releasing all extrinsic motivators. This release of external factors unleashes a boundless energy and love for the game that transports a player into a whole new realm of "feel," experience, and performance.

The outcome of most sporting events in today's world is determined by extrinsic and ego-motivated factors, because that is the state of consciousness in which most of the world lives in the majority of the time. Naturally this state is brought into the sports world by the players and coaches who participate. So at that level, the player and the coaches who can operate best in the ego world, those who have the greatest will to win from an extrinsic standpoint, those who try harder and never give up, will typically prevail. That does not mean, however, that they are experiencing peak performance on the will pathway.

Examples of extrinsic motivation in sports are:
- the desire to win and the fear of losing
- the desire to be superior or dominate and the fear of being inferior and dominated

- the desire for approval and the fear of disapproval
- the desire to be worthy and the fear of being unworthy
- the desire for revenge and the fear of impotence or powerlessness
- the desire for success and the fear of failure

All of these extrinsic motivators have one thing in common. They are based either on a desire to obtain something or a fear or resistance to losing and not attaining something.

Intrinsic motivation, on the other hand, is innate and does not depend on anything outside of the person or athlete. Intrinsic motivation is a natural byproduct of awareness centered consciousness. It just appears and does not have to be programmed or forced into an athlete. Intrinsic motivators are naturally there and are inherent in any life activity including sports and other games. To get a feel for intrinsic motivation, simply observe young children at play. They make up games to engage in before the ego is conditioned to ideas like winning and losing. Children naturally play games for fun and the pure love and enjoyment of them. They set up goals and challenges not to test or measure some idea of who they are or have to be, but rather for the fun of experiencing the game. They immerse themselves in the process of play while being totally present with their actions. They play out of spontaneity and intuitiveness rather than thinking about what they are doing. This is why children have such great motivation and enormous energy for games and can continue to play them for hours and hours without tiring. Children, at least until their indoctrination begins, are not blocked on the *Will* pathway. They are not motivated to play their games by external factors but rather by the inherent intrinsic joy of being and experiencing.

Authentic Sports has discovered that any human activity, including sports, has its own inherent and intrinsic motivators of the Will. They can be accessed simply by releasing all attachments to extrinsic motivation and unblocking a greater amount of energy. Occasionally, an athlete can find solace in sports when things are externally not going well. They can still be inspired by the love of the game.

Kobe Bryant

In 2004, for instance, Kobe Bryant found himself experiencing the most trying of NBA seasons. It was bad enough that a late season shoulder injury kept him from participating in some games while playing with pain in others. Far worse were the horrifying criminal charges that he faced in a Colorado court — charges that he had raped or at least sexually assaulted a nineteen-year-old woman. The shoulder injury could sideline him for a few weeks or months at most. The criminal charges could sideline him for a lifetime.

March 24th promised to be one of the most trying days of all. For the first time since the alleged incident, Bryant would be face to face with his accuser in a Colorado courtroom, watching and listening to her testimony at a preliminary hearing. He would then fly to Los Angeles for a key late season match-up with the Sacramento Kings, not knowing whether he could even make the game in time for the opening tip. Following the game, he would only be able to rest for a few hours before catching another flight back to Colorado for more proceedings in his case. If ever there was a game where Kobe could be expected to lose his focus, the game on the evening of March 24, 2004 would, by all appearances, have been that game.

Bryant took an early morning flight from Newport Beach to Eagle, Colorado, attended the hearing and listened to his accuser testify for over three hours. Following the hearing, he made the two-hour flight back to Los Angeles and arrived in the locker room only forty-five minutes before the game was scheduled to start. Despite the distractions, the lack of preparation time for the game, the pure physical fatigue of a long day in court and two plane rides, and against all odds, Bryant put on one of his best performances of the entire season. We watched the game on television that evening and we noticed from the very start that Kobe seemed to be in a peak performance state. He was inspired, loose, in feel, playing with a freedom and abandonment, and even joy. He made the first two shots of the game, went on to score 36 points, and the Lakers routed the Kings. We were mildly shocked that Bryant could have such an outstanding performance under such stressful circumstances. Curious as to his own explanation, we watched the post-game press conference and heard him talk about his game. What he said caught our attention. While we may not be quoting him verbatim, he said something to this effect: "I just focused back on why I began playing this game in the first place; the smell of the hardwood, the feel of the ball. It's fun to get out on the court and play basketball." Then we understood. Kobe was playing out of love for the game itself and his own prowess. This unleashed an enormous energy in him that allowed him to play without the constraints of any desire to win or fear of losing. He was simply inspired to play basketball.

In that game we believe Bryant found the key to removing the first block on the path to peak performance. He released all attention to extrinsic motivators of his will and allowed his intrinsic motivators to naturally come to the surface. *Authentic Sports* tells this story not to promote, endorse or judge Kobe Bryant`s alleged actions off the court. Rather, we suggest this story illustrates that even under the most stressful external circumstances a player can access the state of peak performance by activating the will through intrinsic motivation.

We have previously mentioned that extrinsic motivation is based in ego-centered consciousness. The ego is motivated by trying to become more while avoiding becoming less. As we said in Chapter 1, the ego is really nothing more than a false sense of self, a "me" that is created by the mind. The mind then believes that it needs to protect or promote this "self." In relative terms, this "me" is very small, fragile, vulnerable and ultimately short-lived. Its constant motivational force is survival and its primary fuel is fear. The ego programs the will to play sports to enhance or inflate its artificial sense of self. It uses the will to see itself as bigger and better than others. The key test for knowing whether you are operating in ego-centered consciousness on the *will* pathway is this: Are you being motivated by desire or resistance? If the answer is yes, you are operating out of ego-centered consciousness or your past programming, and it will probably limit the level of your performance and your enjoyment of the game or any other life activity.

The Ego Performer on the *Will* Pathway

The ego sports performer on the *will* pathway is trapped in the duality domain, the opposing forces of "will" and "won't." It's a desire for "I will get the result I want" and a resistance to "I won't get the result I don't want". As far as the will is concerned in the duality of the ego, every "will" has a "won't." Most coaches try to manufacture and reverse-engineer inspiration with extrinsic motivators to get their players to the "will" and resist the "won't." They are looking at something that is intrinsic or inspired and trying to reverse engineer it through extrinsic motivation. Peak performance really comes from the shift from ego-centered consciousness (the outside) into awareness-centered consciousness (the inside). Awareness-centered consciousness moves beyond the duality of "will' and "won't." The ego performer tries to take the "will" and delete all the "won'ts." It wants the high side without the low side. The ego wants to own and possess motivation.

One trick the ego uses to motivate will is through the double edged sword of praise. In our society, we take it for granted that praise is a good thing. We encourage parents to praise their children and reward them for their success. Parents may offer many external rewards for desired behavior. These rewards can take on many forms such as giving them something like an allowance, ice cream and more TV time. Alternately, parents might motivate their kids by withholding punishment that would otherwise be forthcoming such as "if you clean your room you won't get grounded" or, in the world of sports, "if you make a mistake you're going to run laps" or "you will be taken out of the lineup." There is a subtle but powerful value system communicated to the child through this type of reward/punishment scheme — the child learns to gauge his or her worthiness by external measures: "If I am getting praise then I am worthy and everything is okay. If I am not getting praise, (or even worse, being punished), then I am not worthy and things are not okay." Because this cycle typically begins at a very young age, at some very deep and basic level children learn to believe that their very survival depends upon whether they are being approved of or disapproved of by their parents or primary care givers. Do not underestimate the strength of deep disapproval conditioning! To many, if not most, of us it can trigger the fear of death itself. Approval allows us to temporarily feel some relief from this fear, so we can become addicted to seeking approval.

Praise, then, becomes a form of approval that most of us crave at a deep survival level. The problem is that praise from others is something outside of ourselves (extrinsic), and thus we can never fully count on it, nor can we ever feel secure in it. Praise gives us temporary relief, but in a very short time we feel vulnerable again and need more praise. The desire for praise and approval separates us from our natural intrinsic motivation, short circuiting feel and peak performance.

This dynamic can show up as a trick of the ego on the *Will* pathway. A person can start out with a completely intrinsic motivation to play a game, a pure love of the game itself and enjoyment of the challenge to master it. What often happens is that if the person begins to show some promise of being very "good" at the game by normal external measures, people take notice. People offer praise. Then the person, being vulnerable to the addiction for praise, starts to crave more than just playing the game for its own sake. Suddenly there is tension: "If I don't continue to play this game well, these people won't praise me anymore." The deep-seated survival need for approval has taken over and the joy of the game has been lost. Now the "game" has become serious business. The player has to "work" hard at the game to sustain and improve their level of performance, and thus approval. The game is not fun anymore, and the player who so innocently started to play a game for intrinsic reasons is now completely motivated by external concerns. Burn-out is a common phenomenon for such a player. It is not a stretch to say that one's very sense of identity — who they are — can become inextricably linked to how well they are playing a game. Talk about pressure! Now if they don't play well the survival of who they are (or more accurately, who they believe themselves to be) is threatened. Little wonder that sports can become such a serious grind for many athletes in our society.

Praise, reward and punishment turn an intrinsic internal state into an extrinsic external condition, a mechanical state. This mechanical state depends on outside factors for its motivation. When those outside factors are not present the will becomes depleted with a loss of outside motivation.

Bjorn Borg

Tennis legend Bjorn Borg started playing the pro tour in 1971 at the age of 14. In 1974, just after he turned 18, Borg won the first of his eleven Grand Slams titles at the French Open championships on the red clay of Roland Garros. Between 1974 and 1981 Borg was arguably the best tennis player on the planet. However, in 1981 he lost two Grand Slam finals, Wimbledon and the U.S. Open, to the great American tennis player and future number one, John McEnroe.

Their contrasts in styles of play and temperament made for great entertainment and lead to epic matches. McEnroe, the fiery-tempered serve-and-volley player versus Borg, the Swedish backboard base-liner with incredible topspin strokes and a personality so cool he was known as the "ice man." For some reason, this defeat at the hands of John McEnroe at the U.S. Open seemed to drain motivation from Borg who, at 25 years of age, was in the prime of his career. There were rumors of Borg's ensuing retirement, which came as a great shock to everyone who had followed his career. Borg went on to win the year-ending championships, beating John McEnroe and Ivan Lendl, the future Czech great. Then he simply laid down his racket.

How could somebody quit at the prime of his career with so much to offer the world of tennis? Certainly it was not the fear of losing. *Authentic Sports* suggests that his "ice man" demeanor blocked him from intrinsic motivation, or fun. This, combined with the loss of desire for extrinsic motivations of fame, fortune and the high life, along with the grinding hours of training it took to be the best, lead to Borg's burn-out and loss of will and motivation to continue.

Extrinsic motivation is always based in duality. There is a constant conflict between the high-end of the ego(I will) versus the low-end of the ego(I wont). Life naturally seeks balance, so when the ego sports performer tries to consistently manufacture the high-end of the ego on the *Will* pathway, the low-end of the ego will naturally show up.

Occasionally, an athlete's will is so driven by extrinsic motivators that the athlete can take on a do-or-die attitude. This is a survival instinct of the will at the highest level, the instinct that will often show up when contestants have a hatred for each other.

Ali / Frazier

What is widely considered to be, even by boxing experts, the three greatest fights of all time in the same weight division took place in the early 1970s between the legendary Muhammed Ali and his arch rival, Smokin' Joe Frazier. Ali, a showman who proclaimed himself to be "the greatest," would intentionally antagonize his opponents, both to promote the fight and to get under his opponent's skin. For most opponents, Ali probably won the fight before he stepped into the ring.

Ali`s great boxing abilities, along with his unbelievable confidence, produced too great a challenge for most of his adversaries. His personal attacks on Joe Frazier, such as calling him an "Uncle Tom," a "Gorilla" and other negative comments, made Frazier despise Ali. The attacks became so severe that Frazier's family was threatened by fans who bought into the charade, and his kids were mocked in school. Ali, painting Frazier as an "Uncle Tom," or servant of white people, caused Frazier to be ostracized by the black community. Frazier felt that he would rather die in the ring than lose to Ali. No matter how much punishment he endured, he was going to keep coming at Ali like a gladiator fighting to the death. This will to win at any price lead to three wars in the ring that are still talked about today as epic battles of survival. To the very end, just before his death, Joe Frazier had an animosity towards Muhammad Ali – a bitterness that he simply couldn't let go of. *Authentic Sports* views even the highest motivation of the ego as a destructive force.

High extrinsic motivation can be observed in extreme sports such as cliff jumping, big wave surfing, tight rope walking or any other contest wherein an athlete's life is put at risk. These sports draw upon our strongest instinctual mechanism — the flight or fight response. When survival is on the line through extreme risk-taking, the mind/body will sometimes move into a peak performance state. This shock into the present moment often transcends an extreme athlete's ordinary levels of athletic aptitude. The extreme sport athlete is engulfed in an effort to overcome fear, or the flight response, through the high-risk activity revolving around life or death. Like a drug used to produce altered states of consciousness, the adrenalin rush of overcoming the fear of death becomes an addiction. This, however, can be another trick of the ego, because the ego is really just trying to overcome itself.

The fight or flight response is just two sides of the same ego coin. One side is fight — overcome and conquer your fears. The other side is flight — quit and give in to your fears. In primitive times, both sides were equally valuable for surviving. Hunting (fight) for wild game or running (flight) from a lion is just one example. In today's culture the fight response is considered a strength, and therefore more valuable. The flight response is looked down upon as a weakness. The truth is that they both exist on the same level of consciousness.

The Authentic Sports Performer on the Will Pathway

The *Authentic Sports* performer's will is free to experience sports through a unified (non-dualistic) state. She does not divide energy between "will" and "won't." She is free from the tug of war between opposing opposites. Inspiration is the natural state of the authentic performer. It is not necessary to try to "get up" for a sporting event. *Authentic Sports* performers, experiencing sports through awareness-centered consciousness, are intrinsically motivated, with inspiration being a natural by-product. This creative *feel* state allows the will to channel motivational energy freely from unlimited internal reservoirs. The will is not dependent on anything external for its motivation.

What about Goals?

At this point you might be saying to yourself, "Okay, this sounds great. But if I don't have any external motivators or goals, won't I just be drifting aimlessly without any point to playing the game at all?" You may be conjuring up an image of yourself blissfully swatting at a tennis ball without a care in the world as to whether the ball lands in the court or up in the stands. Doesn't all of this talk about eliminating extrinsic motivators leave you without a purpose for playing the game? After all, every game is designed with an external purpose —to put the ball in the basket, to cross the goal line or to get to home plate. All games have some external measure for how they are being played. Points are awarded for certain activities and the points determine the outcome of the game. How can one possibly play a game without any purpose at all, without being motivated by extrinsic factors that dictate the objectives of the game?

Here we must draw a distinction between paying attention to and being mindful of the purposes and objectives of a game and actually drawing motivating energy from it. Every game has objectives. Much of the fun of playing games is in the challenge of playing at a higher and higher level. The game sets forth reference points for determining how well you are meeting its objectives. In golf, for example, the objective of the game is to get the ball into the cup with the fewest number of strokes. Each hole is assigned a "par" value as a reference point for its objective. In large part, the golfer measures progress in the mastery of the game by how many strokes he or she takes in a round of golf.

The intrinsic motivator for playing a game is to enjoy the challenge of meeting and mastering the game's stated objectives. Being intrinsically motivated by playing a game is a deliberate activity. The will is directing its energy toward an objective. But *why* the will is doing so determines whether that energy can freely flow toward the mastery of the game, rather than being blocked by extrinsic factors that are not inherent in playing. One can be completely mindful of the game's objectives and completely focused on attaining them without having the ego being motivated by extrinsic factors such as being too attached to the outcome.

When attention is placed on both the objectives inherent in the game and on self-mastery in pursuing those objectives, there is an unlimited source of energy and inspiration leading to pure enjoyment. That is why we play games in the first place. But when attention is placed on the objectives of the game for ego-based reasons ("This shows that I am worthy or special or better than you!") energy is quickly drained and "feel" is blocked by the ensuing tension. The *Will* pathway's focus is about the source from whence energy and feel is being derived. Extrinsic motivators derive energy and feel from the limited confines of the world "out there," which ultimately cannot sustain a high level of play for very long. Intrinsic motivators derive energy and feel from the source of life itself. In the absence of ego, boundless energy is available.

"Accidental" Peak Performance

Sometimes inspirational energy of the will can be accessed accidentally. Our observation is that occasionally certain teams or players will fall into a peak performance state that transcends the normal dualistic world of the ego-sports performer and play at a higher level than they normally would play. This can come about through a variety of factors that occasionally, and usually by surprise, knock the ego off of its pedestal, releasing the natural energy of intrinsic motivation.

Tom Weiskopf

Tom Weiskopf was a talented golfer that played in the late 1960s and 70s. He was a few years younger than Jack Nicklaus and many saw him as the heir apparent to Nicklaus` throne. Tremendous expectations were heaped upon him, which unfortunately set him up for having his attention directed towards extrinsic motivators. But Weiskopf, somewhat like Greg Norman in later years, always seemed to fall a shot short in the major championships of golf. Whenever he had a head-to-head duel with Nicklaus, Nicklaus almost always seemed to prevail. In 1973, however, Weiskopf`s father passed away and something happened to Tom. He suddenly went on a streak, winning several tournaments that culminated in his first major championship victory in the British Open at Troon.

What happened to Weiskopf that so radically lifted his level of play? He likely had been capable of this type of play for many years, but something inside of him shifted. We wonder whether the death of Tom's father caused his ego to suddenly take a back seat to his true love of the game and the original intrinsic motivators that caused him to play the game when he was a boy. The death of a loved one often has the effect of shocking the ego into submission. When his dad died, Weiskopf may have suddenly realized that all the things that his ego had been worried about in the extrinsic world meant nothing at all. When he released all of the tension that he had been carrying caused by the extrinsic trappings of being a star golf professional (and particularly all of the external expectations that had been heaped upon him), he was free to just play golf. And play he did, with great feel, joy, and fun! Ironically, when he stopped being motivated by external things his performance by external measures greatly improved and undoubtedly his pure enjoyment of playing the game improved as well.

Unfortunately, Weiskopf was not able to sustain this level of play for very long. After some period of time we suspect that his old habits and extrinsic motivators kicked back in, and he went back to being the "bridesmaid" at many major tournaments. Fortunately, a player does not need to suffer a life tragedy in order to quiet ego-based extrinsic motivators and access the natural intrinsic motivators that lie within. Rather, they can do so by simply becoming aware of the extrinsic motivators that are at work. A simple question to ask is, "What am I trying to get out of this?" The answer could be any number of things, such as:

"I'm trying to prove myself to others"
"I'm trying to avoid being embarrassed"
"I'm trying to 'be' somebody"
"I'm trying to win"
"I'm trying not to lose"
"I'm trying to look good"

"I'm trying not to look bad"

The list could go on and on. Notice that each one of these answers contains the element of desiring or resisting something "out there," a sure sign that ego-centered consciousness is at work.

Authentic Sports performance suggests that inspirational play does not have to happen only now and then. It does not take some kind of conditioning or training over years or to be a professional athlete to have an inspired will. Inspiration can be accessed deliberately, simply by being aware of intrinsic motivation.

Jimmy Valvano

A story that illustrates the pinnacle of the will is the inspiring story of the former great N.C State coach and humanitarian Jimmy Valvano. Inspiration is the highest quality of the will in awareness centered consciousness. It transcends selflessness and personal motivation. Perhaps the most improbable, unbelievable, and inspiring run to the NCAA basketball championships occurred in 1983. The team was the North Carolina State Wolfpack led by their inspirational coach Jimmy Valvano, known as Jimmy V. The essence of this story, however, is not about all the miraculous close games NC State had to win in order to fulfill the dream of cutting the nets down in the NCAA championship game. These include unlikely wins over North Carolina with Michael Jordon, Virginia with Ralph Sampson, and Houston with Akeem Olajuwon. The essence of this story is about determination, inspiration and a higher calling.

Jimmy V was an outgoing, enthusiastic, and passionate basketball coach from New York. Dreaming of one day cutting down the nets at the NCAA championships, he would have his players cut down the nets at practice. He would have his players do this for the purpose of rehearsing it or making it seem real and to instill his conviction and dream into his players. He told his players that before they graduate that they would cut down the nets and be NCAA champions.

During NC States incredible run throughout the NCAA tournament Jimmy V`s love for basketball and his players was clear to see for all who watched. His never give up attitude was contagious and was witnessed in his teams many come from behind victories. His players did not seem to feel the normal tension associated with the desire to win and the resistance to losing, allowing for inspired play. Little did Jimmy V know that his motto of never give up would inspire others way beyond the basketball court.

Jimmy V retired from coaching basketball a few tumultuous years after the NC State Championship season. Allegations that his players accepted money and that their grades were altered to allow them to play were threatening his reputation. Jimmy V turned his attention to TV, becoming a basketball analyst. His engaging, colorful style, and enthusiasm for the game made him an instant success. As life can never be fully known or understood through the logical or rational mind, Jimmy V contracted terminal cancer and was given 10 months to live. During his fight for survival, Jimmy V never lost hope for a cure. His never give up attitude was put to its greatest test.

During his many visits and time at Duke University hospital he became very close friends with the legendary Duke coach Mike Krzyzewski. Jimmy V and Mike talked about carrying on the battle to find a cure for cancer by forming a foundation. During his final months of life the Jimmy V foundation, a charity for cancer research was born and his legacy lives on. The Jimmy V foundation has raised more than 100 million dollars for the fight against cancer. On March 3rd 1993 Jimmy V gave a speech at the Espy`s which inspired and moved many people in the audience to tears. The speech ended with this inspiring message "cancer can take away all of my physical abilities. It cannot touch my mind, it cannot touch my heart, and it cannot touch my soul. And those 3 things are going to live on forever."

Jimmy V believed that one day he would win the fight against cancer although it may not be for himself. Authentic sports suggests that Jimmy V was destined to help millions of people through his inspired will and his transforming motto of "Don't give up, don't ever give up." We believe that Jimmy V had a higher calling to serve humanity. Jimmy V died April 28, 1993. Words that he lived by are etched on his tombstone-"Take time every day to laugh, to think, to cry." He faced life and death with class, dignity, humor, humility and an inspired will.

Now that you have discovered that inspiration is the key to the *Will*, the next pathway where the energy and feel required for peak performance can be blocked is the *Belief* pathway. Let's discover together the ability to transcend limiting beliefs and negative self-image. Welcome to the power of faith and the realm of all possibilities!

Chapter 3
Belief: Pathway to the Realm of all Possibilities

Beliefs act as filters through which we perceive and experience reality. They are the primary influence on an athlete's thoughts and actions. Beliefs, in general, condition our personal reality. *Authentic Sports* refers to *Belief* as "an internal parameter through which an athlete will allow himself or herself to perform." What an athlete believes influences the quality of his or her performance.

Beliefs are a byproduct of an individual's level of consciousness. When an athlete is connected to lower levels of consciousness, his or her beliefs are conditioned, programmed, and reside in the domain of duality. The athlete's beliefs reside in the opposing opposites of "can' and "can't." When an athlete is connected to higher levels of consciousness, belief is connected to source energy. In the higher levels of consciousness an athlete is connected to faith, and experiences the realm of all possibilities.

Beliefs on the lower levels of consciousness become programmed thought forms which restrict an athlete's performance. On higher levels of consciousness the unknown, or *feel*, transcends the limitations of belief. The most fundamental belief about yourself is your idea of who you are (self-image). This has an enormous impact on the level at which you allow yourself to play. Your beliefs about yourself are either conditioned through ego-centered consciousness or created through the realm of all possibilities in awareness-centered consciousness.

Ego-Centered Consciousness on the Belief Pathway

In ego-centered consciousness, beliefs are indoctrinated, conditioned, and programmed. An athlete's belief can be indoctrinated early on by parents and later influenced by teachers, peers and coaches. Some athletes form beliefs as a response to an antagonistic person and take on a rebellious attitude when it comes to conforming to authority. Regardless of where the athlete's beliefs come from, beliefs formed in ego-centered consciousness become a force of habit which do not adapt to the constantly changing environment of sports performance. These habits, stuck in the duality of "can" and "can't," lead to over-control, doubt, trying too hard and the arch enemy of sports performance, tension or restricted feel.

Tension caused by an athlete's desire for "I can," and resistance to "I can't," decreases the availability of energy and feel needed for peak performance.

Beliefs which were formed early in childhood can become a barrier to sports performance as an adult. Beliefs such as "I will never be good enough," or "my parents and coaches don't believe in me," can be hidden influences throughout an athlete's career. All beliefs in ego-centered consciousness, by their nature, are limiting and reflect a limited point of view of human potential.

Beliefs divide attention between what you think you can do and what you think you can't do. This programs the parameters within an athlete's consciousness through which they experience their performance. Beliefs, by their very nature, are self-fulfilling paradigms which limit human potential. Athletes tend to produce a performance which matches up with their self-image or self-belief. This programs a constant tension between the athlete and his beliefs about himself.

An illustration of how limiting beliefs about the capabilities of an athlete's body can be challenging for an athlete to overcome can be observed in NFL combines. Nowhere is evaluating an athlete based on their physical attributes more on display. NFL combines measure every physical aspect of an aspiring professional football player. The measure of a football player's speed, height, weight, vertical leap, strength, and agility can make or break his career chances. Many coaches and scouts have misjudged talent based on these measurements or physical attributes. Jerry Rice, for instance, the all-time leading receiver in yardage, was said to be too slow to play wide receiver in the NFL. Emmitt Smith, the all-time leading rusher, was believed to be too small to take the pounding a running back endures in the NFL.

Kurt Warner

An NFL story that shows how talent and physical ability can be misjudged based on limited beliefs is the story of NFL great, and future Hall of Fame quarterback, Kurt Warner. Warner was undrafted in 1994, and although he got a tryout with the Green Bay Packers he was released before the regular season started. While it appeared that the NFL did not believe in Kurt Warner, Warner believed in himself.

To keep his dream alive, Warner signed an arena football league contract with the Iowa Barnstormers in 1995. He also worked as a graduate assistant coach for Northern Iowa University and bagged groceries at Hy-Vee grocery store in Cedar Falls Iowa for $5.50 an hour. People of less belief and character would have given up on their dream of being an NFL quarterback. In 1997 Kurt Warner underwent a religious conversion. *Authentic Sports* suggests that this belief in a power greater than himself strengthened his inner conviction and kept him on the path to fulfill his dream.

In 1998, Warner signed his first NFL contract with the talented and emotional coach Dick Vermeil and the St. Louis Rams. Vermeil, who had experienced a loss as coach of the Philadelphia Eagles in the 1980 Super Bowl, was also looking for another chance at redemption. Warner was allocated to NFL Europe with the Amsterdam Admirals where he became a star player and led the league in passing yards and touchdowns. In 1999 he was brought back to the Rams and signed to be a backup quarterback behind the newly acquired Trent Green. As fate would have it, Trent Green tore his ACL and Warner was thrust into the spotlight. Dick Vermeil is famously quoted as saying, "We will rally around Kurt and play good football." It is unlikely, at that time, that he realized that his St. Louis Rams were about to become Super Bowl champions.

Warner put together one of the top seasons in NFL history, throwing for 4,353 yards and 41 touchdowns, with a completion rate of 65.1%. The Rams high-powered offense, under offensive coordinator Mike March, became known as the "greatest show on turf." Warner went on to win the 1999 regular season MVP award and he led the Rams to a Super Bowl XXXIV championship in 2000 over the Tennessee Titans. He also won Super Bowl MVP honors for his outstanding performance. Other accomplishments in Warner's career include the 2001 league MVP award and two other Super Bowl appearances, one with the Rams in 2001 the other with the Arizona Cardinals in 2008.

Major highlights in Warner's career include the seventh highest career passing rating and the second highest career completion percentage in NFL history. In 13 overall playoff games he ranks first in completion percentage at 66.5%.

There is a growing tendency among coaches and trainers to overly rely on factors such as past background, genetics, past performances and age determinants when it comes to evaluating an athlete's potential. These factors do not take into consideration the unseen potential to transcend the limiting labels and beliefs of the so-called experts. How many times have we witnessed, as fans, an athlete who is not given much of a chance to do great things go on to astonish the experts?

Dara Torres

In the world of women's swimming, for instance, the age of 30 is considered to be too old to be competitive against swimmers in their late teens and early twenty's. Yet Dara Torres, a wife and mother, at the age of 40 transcended this belief by winning the 50 meter freestyle and breaking the U. S. record at the Nationals in Indianapolis, Ind. Her victory qualified her for the Beijing Olympics in 2008. Then, at the age of 41, she won three silver medals and barely missed the gold medal in the 50 meter freestyle. So much for the age barrier!

Awareness-Centered Consciousness on the Belief Pathway

In awareness-centered consciousness, beliefs are deliberate, creative, and present-moment oriented. They are free from past limitations and remain open and receptive to the infinite possibilities of the present. There are no limiting beliefs that keep you stuck in a conditioned program that is not working.

Beliefs in awareness-centered consciousness adapt moment-to-moment to the conditions within the sporting environment. Beliefs are not fixed, so there is no tension created between the duality of "can" and "can't." Present moment awareness is creative and flexible. It is not conditioned by past experiences. There is a lack of struggle, trying, over-control and accompanying tension or restricted feel, which are byproducts of ego-centered beliefs. Accessing this neutral state of suspended belief allows energy and feel to flow freely towards the realm of all possibilities. When an athlete enters this realm, there are no barriers to athletic performance due to earlier past programming.

Awareness-centered consciousness, or the "observation state," removes ego and limited, or conditioned beliefs. There is an expanded feeling based on the assumption that anything is possible. Attention is not divided, which allows performance to improve and evolve. The athlete's performance is free to move to higher levels because there are no fixed beliefs or limited self-image. Belief is transformed into faith, which allows the athlete to enter the unknown with all its infinite possibilities. Faith is a state of unlimited belief. When you release limited beliefs and expand into limitless possibilities (faith), more empowering beliefs become available to you because you have tapped into a higher state of consciousness.

Wilma Rudolph

An inspirational story of faith and transforming limiting beliefs is that of Wilma Rudolph. Rudolph was an African American track and field star. She was born prematurely in the "Volunteer State" of Tennessee, weighing only 4.5 pounds, in 1940. The medical field then was not as advanced as it is today and her survival chances where unknown. She was the 20th of 22 children and came from a very poor family. As a very young child she was sickly, catching the measles, mumps, and chicken pox. At the age of four she caught both double pneumonia and scarlet fever. It became noticeable that her left foot and leg were growing weak and deformed. Doctors decided that she must have contracted polio, a crippling disease, and would probably never walk again.

While the doctors might have believed this crippling disease was Wilma Rudolph's fate, her mother's faith transcended conventional medical belief. She told Wilma that she could do anything she wanted to in life. She took her to Meharry Hospital at Fisk University in Tennessee. There, Wilma's mother was taught physical therapy techniques and she, along with other members of her family, worked on Wilma's leg. It began to get stronger. At the age of 12 Wilma Rudolph took off her leg brace and walked down the aisle of her church. She was now able to walk without crutches, leg braces, or corrective shoes. Her determination and faith, as well as that of her family, had brought Wilma this far, but what happened next defies imagination.

Wilma decided that she wanted to be the world's greatest female runner. In her first race in high school, at the age of thirteen, she came in dead last. There would be many more races in which Wilma would not fare too well, but her faith, spirit, and inner conviction kept her moving toward her goal. Wilma eventually started to win races, and once she did, she kept on winning. At the age of sixteen she qualified for the 1956 Olympic Games and won a bronze medal in the 4x100 relay. But she had not yet hit her stride.

She ran track, on a full track scholarship, at Tennessee State University where she met track coach Ed Temple, the man who would become her mentor and train her for the 1960 Olympics in Rome. In that year, with Ed Temple at her side, Wilma Rudolph accomplished that which, based on her childhood disabilities, seemed to be the impossible. She won three Olympic gold medals, beating the great German sprinter Yetta Heine in the 100 and 200 meters. She also won a gold medal, anchoring the 4x100 meter relay.

Wilma Rudolph has credited her faith and positive thinking for her amazing Olympic victories, demonstrating that when you tap into the power of faith, energy is unblocked and aligns to your core intention.

The Ego Performer on the Belief Pathway

The ego sports performer is trapped in the duality domain, somewhere between "can" and "can't," low self-esteem, and asserted high self-belief (arrogance). They are stuck between negative and positive beliefs such as inferior ("I suck") and superior ("I am the greatest"). If athletes believe they are the greatest player in the world they have some idea or image of how great that is. That belief may be limiting them from truly performing at their very highest level, even if they are better at their position or sport than everyone else. All beliefs are somewhat limiting by their very nature. When an athlete's performance slips below the level of which he or she believes they are capable, they manifest tension, and will tend to find a way to get their performance back to a comfortable or average level. By the same token, if an athlete's performance rises above the level the athlete believes he or she is capable of performing, this also manifests tension, and the athlete will find a way to cool off his or her performance to get back into the ego's comfort zone.

The ego performer believes that the high end of the ego is the way to peak performance. So the ego tries to reverse-engineer beliefs to obtain the highest level of sporting excellence, discounting consciousness and feel as the real cause of peak performance. Positive or unlimited beliefs occur naturally and in effect when an athlete is in awareness-centered consciousness. Ego performers see positive beliefs as the cause of peak performance, so they try to possess them when, in reality, awareness-centered consciousness caused the positive beliefs which led to the peak performance. When beliefs are created through awareness-centered consciousness, we call them *authentic* beliefs.

The ego's attempt to manufacture positive beliefs in order to program peak performance is just another way it desires to replicate natural processes by working backwards (reverse-engineering) from the result. It is the ego, back to its old tricks of wanting one side of the ego coin without the other — wanting the "can" without the "can't" — and wanting superior without inferior. When a performance takes place in the duality domain of ego-centered consciousness on the belief pathway, sometimes an athlete's belief starts off with "I can win" only to later turn into "I can't win." One story demonstrating this concerns tennis great, Olympic gold medalist, hall of fame inductee, and 8 time grand slam winner Andre Agassi.

Andre Agassi

For Andre Agassi, reaching the 2005 U.S open finals in New York at the age of 35 was a remarkable achievement. Winning 6 rounds of tennis matches against much younger opponents was inspiring to the thousands of people cheering in the stands as well as the millions more around the world applauding from their couches. Agassi needed just one more win to make history and become one of the oldest players ever to win a singles title at the US open. However, waiting in the finals was Roger Federer, the defending U.S open champion and a man already being regarded by many as one of, if not the greatest, player of all time. So the stage was set for this highly anticipated and dramatic match-up between Roger Federer, an immensely talented all-court player in his prime, and Andre Agassi, an aggressive base liner nearing the end of his career.

The U.S open finals of 2005 began with Federer winning a hard fought first set 6 games to 3 over Agassi. One could see, though, that both players were playing at an extremely high level, with very few unforced errors and many great exchanges. Agassi outplayed Federer, winning the second set six games to two. The third set, which is very often the decisive set in a best out of five set match, went back and forth with both players making incredible shots. It finally went into a tiebreaker, in which Federer seemed to be re-energized, lifting his level up a notch. He won it easily, seven points to one. In the fourth set it seemed evident that Agassi`s spirit and game had been broken following that third set tiebreaker, and Federer cruised to a six games to one victory, thus making him the 2005 U.S open champion.

After watching that fourth set of the match, we began to wonder why Agassi's game collapsed in the fourth set. Was he injured? Did Federer simply take his game to a new level? Or was there another answer? In the post-match interview Agassi conceded that he believed Federer to be the best player he had ever played against and had decided he would have had to play perfect tennis just to have a chance of beating him. So could Agassi's collapse in the fourth set have had something to do with his belief that Federer was unbeatable on this day? After losing the third set tiebreaker did he succumb to the belief that he really had no chance of winning? We propose that Agassi played the first three sets from an "I can win level" on the belief pathway. He was confident in his ability leading to a high level of performance. In the fourth set he descended into a lower level, or low end of the ego, on the belief pathway, thinking, in effect, "I can't win." This limiting belief about what is possible restricted his performance and feel leading to an uncompetitive fourth set.

Sometimes a top athletic performer will program the ego to a delusional state where they believe they cannot be beaten. Oddly enough, embracing vulnerability is more a sign of strength than of weakness and ultimately enhances an athlete's performance rather than detracting from it. These asserted programmed beliefs can make an athlete feel invincible, leading to under-training and over-confidence. One such story concerns a boxer who would become one of the most well-known and feared names in boxing history.

Mike Tyson

Nearly every opponent who ever faced "Iron" Mike Tyson in the ring confesses to feeling the intense power of his punches. Many ended up unconscious on the canvas. Tyson's sheer destructiveness inside the boxing ring was sometimes mirrored by his violent behavior outside its ropes. Tyson's brushes with the law and what was described by some as his "train wreck" of a life unfolded for the whole world to see. Even those who were not fans of boxing knew who Mike Tyson was, as much for his public antics and violent life as for his boxing skills.

Tyson gave many interviews throughout the years, providing a glimpse into his beliefs surrounding his behavior both inside and outside the ring. It seems as though his self-beliefs may have crossed over from merely a natural confidence in his own abilities to arrogance and cockiness. The young fighter believed he was unbeatable. He once referred to himself as "the baddest man on the planet." Of course, this kind of claim was nothing new in the world of boxing. Mohammed Ali was famous for promoting his fights by making such arrogant claims. Tyson, however, seemed different. It seemed as though Tyson actually believed he was invincible.

Any belief, whether it be positive or negative, that arises from the ego will ultimately lead to failure. This failure is not easily measured by the number of times an athlete wins or loses. It is demonstrated rather in the quality of their own consciousness, because the quality of one's consciousness is the true measure of success.

Tyson's asserted belief in his own invincibility ultimately led to his failure both inside the ring and within his personal life. In February of 1990 he was the heavy weight champion of the world. He boasted a record of 37 wins and no defeats. On February 11th of the same year, in Tokyo Japan, Tyson took on Buster Douglas, a 42-1 underdog journeyman fighter with a record of 29 wins and 4 defeats. Going into the fight, gamblers were not betting on who would win, but in which round Tyson would knock Douglas out. The fight ended up becoming one of the most famous in history because the 10th round did not conclude with Douglas lying on the canvas. Instead, the heavy weight champion of the world, Mike Tyson, was not able to continue. The undefeated champion of the world lay bloodied on the canvas, just as many of his previous opponents had been. Tyson later admitted that he had not prepared properly for this fight and that he had completely underestimated Buster Douglas` fighting abilities, possibly caused by Tyson's overestimation of his own. This was not Tyson's only failure in life. He had many more within his personal life. One of the most notable was his rape conviction in 1992, after which he served three years in prison.

Overestimating or underestimating one's own athletic abilities is a byproduct of ego-centered consciousness on the belief pathway. A personal perception of either one's self or one's opponent becomes clouded and will be influenced by the ego beliefs held. In awareness-centered consciousness one is free of these self-centered beliefs.

The Authentic Performer on the Belief Pathway

The authentic performer on the belief pathway perceives sports performance through awareness-centered consciousness. This observer state of consciousness removes ego and neutralizes duality. The authentic sports performer does not limit her performance through the duality domain of "can" and "can't" or any other self-limiting beliefs. Since there is no separation or judgment involved in observation, there is no energy or feel being blocked, because she is not concerned with whether she is better or worse than her opponents.

For the authentic sports performer, there is no average or fixed performance level based on some type of limited belief, so there is no resistance to anything being experienced. She is immersed in the process through faith, without being preoccupied by beliefs. She neutralizes the ego on the belief pathway accessing faith and experiences the realm of all possibilities.

Roger Bannister

Roger Bannister, the great English runner, was the first man to run a mile in less than four minutes. He had faith that this feat was possible. There was a collective belief, at that time, that there was no way of breaking the four minute mile. The old record of four minutes and 1.4 seconds had been in the record books for nine years. Sports reporters claimed that breaking the four minute mile barrier was impossible. There were even doctors who believed that running under a four minute mile could lead to physical death.

Bannister realized that the main reason the four minute mile had not been broken was that World War II had interrupted track competition between the combative nations. He believed that in the nine-year period between 1945 and 1954 the mile record would have been broken, if not for the war.

On May 6, 1954 in a meet between British AAA and Oxford University, track history was about to be made. On the Iffley Road track in Oxford, England, Bannister ran the mile in 3 minutes and 59.4 seconds. The track meet was broadcast live on the BBC radio and likely produced quite a stir around the world. Bannister had accomplished the impossible!

When human limits are surpassed, the consciousness and performance of athletes all over the world is elevated. This is the effect of breaking a collective belief, highlighting the fact that human potential is not limited by records and beliefs. Roger Bannister's breaking of this long-standing record was not because he was overconfident or arrogant, but rather because he entered the realm of all possibility, where beliefs are not an issue.

The "Miracle On Ice"

One of the most incredible stories of overcoming odds and entering the realm of all possibilities took place in the 1980 winter Olympics in Lake Placid, New York. This incredible hockey match became known as the "miracle on ice". Herb Brooks, the coach of the US hockey squad, had put together a collection of college players who were not even considered to be the best available collegiate talent in the U.S. Nine of his players came from the University of Minnesota, where Brooks had coached. Four members of the team came from Boston University. Brooks believed that to beat the Russians he needed players with great team speed who could keep up with the Russians and wear them down. By constantly bringing in new, fresh players, he believed that he could pull off a miraculous upset.

The U.S entered the medal round, competing against the highly touted Soviet team, with a chance to play for the Gold medal. The Soviets, whom many experts considered to be the best in the world, were really a collection of professional players who were advertised as amateurs. They played and trained together on a year-round basis and were subsidized by the government. They were 3-1 against NHL professional teams in exhibition hockey games and routed the NHL all-stars 6-0 to win the challenge cup. On February 9, 1980 the Soviet team defeated the US squad 10-3 in an exhibition game. Later the Soviet coach said that this led to overconfidence on the part of the Soviet hockey team who already may have believed they were unbeatable. On Friday, February 22, the U.S hockey team took the ice against a team that had won the Olympic Gold medal in the 1964, 1968, 1972, and 1976 Olympics. During that stretch of time, they had amassed a record of 27-1-1, outscoring their opponents 175-44. Before the match began, Herb Brooks pulled out a note he had written on a piece of paper and read it to his team: "You were born to be a player, you were meant to be here, this moment is yours." Brooks may have believed that the Soviet team might beat his team 99 out of 100 times, but this night was theirs.

The U.S hockey team rotated in fresh players constantly. With Jim Craig as goalie, they held off the Soviet attack and were able to defeat the Soviets 4-3. At the moment they won the game the famous sports announcer Al Michaels shouted one of the most famous lines in sports history: "Do you believe in miracles?" The "miracle on ice" was voted the top sports moment of the 20th century by Sports Illustrated. The famous sports reporter and announcer, Jim McKay, compared this upset to a Canadian college football team defeating the Pittsburgh Steelers who were then the current Super Bowl champions.

The American team went on to win the Gold medal, but defeating the Soviet team was clearly a peak performance experience. They demonstrated the power of faith leading to the realm of all possibilities.

Once limiting beliefs have been suspended and neutralized, the next place energy and feel can be restricted and inhibited is in the Mental Pathway. Let's discover together the unlimited potential of free mind. Welcome to the power of the present!

Chapter 4
Mental: Pathway to Freedom

The mind, in relationship to sports performance, processes information and gives the body direction and feedback based on the senses. The mind is a medium through which consciousness is perceived and experienced. It can perceive sports through lower levels of consciousness — ego-centered consciousness, or higher level of consciousness — awareness-centered consciousness. When an athlete operates on lower levels of consciousness the mind is conditioned, or programmed, and resides in the duality domain of "attach" or "repel." It either attaches to what it desires, or repels what it resists. For example, an athlete may be attached to doing the action right and resists doing the action wrong — in other words, making mistakes. This leads to mental tension and restricted feel and performance. If this mental tension becomes too great, an athlete's mind may become overwhelmed, leading to withdrawing attention from the task at hand - not caring about the outcome, or just going through the motions, otherwise known as tanking.

Ego-Centered Consciousness on the Mental Pathway

The mind in ego-centered consciousness becomes a conditioned memory program (the known). It processes information subjectively through the inner voice of judgment. The mind resembles a mechanical system in which it perceives and identifies through past recorded experiences. It reads the conditioned program and repeats it in the future, becoming a kind of broken record wherein the sports performance is replicated and "stuck" at previous levels.

The mind, in ego-centered consciousness, only deals with the known (programming). There is a mind/body separation which disconnects the athlete from the present moment, the natural feeling state. This makes the athlete act solely from a conditioned program which lacks flexibility, adaptability and creativeness. The mind is only used to process information based on its past programming and relationship to the results. It is attached to good results and resists bad results. This tango of opposing opposites creates struggle and over-control.

In ego-centered consciousness the mind becomes emphasized on concentration or forced focus, leading to excessive effort, excessive tension, and a restriction of feel. Attention can become fixed on distractions such as the opponent, conditions of contests, rain, noise, heat, cold, or the score. The mind becomes sticky, totally attached to those things outside of its control. It can condition an internal self-criticism, "the voice of judgment." This constant chatter or internal dialogue of the "monkey mind" does not allow for focus in the present moment.

Ego-centered consciousness on the mental pathway kidnaps the authentic self (the unconditioned self) and replaces it with its ego identity. This identity theft deals with each moment through mental-emotional reactive patterns which have been previously conditioned. The mind becomes cluttered with thinking, analyzing and judging, or not allowing the space for creativity to take place. New feedback that could enhance the feel of sports performance becomes unnoticed by the mind. The athlete becomes a prisoner of his or her thoughts rather than being immersed in the task at hand. Over-thinking and analysis leads to less feel, less intuitiveness, and less spontaneity in the athlete's performance. On the mental pathway, in ego-centered consciousness, the mind is absorbed in thinking, and the energy and feel for peak performance is blocked.

Awareness-Centered Consciousness on the Mental Pathway

When the mind shifts into awareness-centered consciousness, the observation state removes ego, which bypasses the thought program - duality and opposing opposites. This observation state is your authentic self, the self beyond any conditioned program. The mind in observation state is not conditioned by desire and resistance, but remains in a neutral state of acceptance that is never in conflict with what *is*. When the mind is in this state all mistakes are treated as teachers, welcome guides for improving sports performance and personal feel. There is no failure — only feedback. Mistakes are not taken personally.

When the mind is in awareness-centered consciousness there is an intense focus on the process. Every action is performed with undivided attention both effectively and efficiently. The mind processes information (the known) from the unknown (feel). For example, the athlete feels a high level of anticipation of what is going to happen (the known) before it happens (the unknown). The phenomenon known as "beginner's luck" works off the principle that the mind is capable of envisioning and connecting to a skilled performance when it is centered in awareness. The absolute beginner has no idea what is going to happen (the unknown) and can experience a remarkable performance that cannot be attributed to any kind of skill or training. The phenomenon of beginner's luck is often short-lived because the thinking mind interrupts the process, the flow of feel to form.

Daniel's Experience

One such short story of beginner's luck took place when I was in college. While joking around with a couple of friends in a game room at the University of West Florida, I convinced them that my roommate was a professional pool player and I challenged them to a game against him. In reality, my roommate was a novice pool player with very little experience and no training at all. My friends, of course, were not convinced that my roommate was a pro and were anxious to take the challenge. As I walked back to the dorm, I wondered how I was going to pull this off and if my roommate would go along with a pool match challenge.

He agreed, as a gag, to pretend that he was a professional and to keep up the charade as long as we could. Obviously on his first bad shot the cat would be out of the bag. What happened next should probably be written up in Ripley's *Believe It or Not.* My roommate walked in with the type of swagger that would be associated with a professional pool player. He approached the table very carefully, chose a pool stick, and examined the pool table and the roll of the ball for any imperfections that could interfere with his execution. My friends who had accepted the challenge watched him intently, seemingly mesmerized by how deliberate he was going about his preparation. We gave them the advantage of breaking first and of course, as luck would have it, no balls went into the pockets. My roommate moved to the table relaxed and deliberate, chalked his stick confidently...and proceeded to run the table!

The opponents, facing a man whom they now believed to be a professional, were in shock at his performance and had no desire to compete against him again. On the way back to the dorm, my roommate admitted that he had never sunk more than two balls in a row. The combination of my roommate's detachment to the known (the result), doing something just for pure fun, and connecting himself to a "feel," or visual impression of a professional pool player, lead to a peak performance experience. The mind, working through the unknown, unified feel (empty mind) with form (body) creating a mind/body sync. This merges an athlete with the task-relevant action of sports while, at the same time, connecting him to the nature of the game.

In awareness-centered consciousness the mind processes information objectively in a non-judgmental way. There is a lack of mental tension and therefore an ease and effortlessness to athletic action. There is a relaxed, intensive, one-pointed attention in each moment. This is often referred to as *mindfulness*. Mindfulness is passive in that it does not require any effort or trying. It is a natural byproduct of awareness-centered consciousness or observation.

In awareness-centered consciousness the mind is free from distractions either internally (self-criticism or analysis) or externally (the score, approval). It is in a neutral state, free-flowing in the present moment, and adapts to the constant change of the sporting environment. The mind is receptive and responsive rather than fixed and reactive. Thinking serves awareness. The mind remains open to the uniqueness of each moment and responds to it based on what is needed at the time. It notices, or observes, and takes into account the minutest detail of the athletic experience.

All feedback necessary to enhance sports performance is observed and processed in awareness-centered consciousness. The mind naturally corrects any previously made mistakes. It is in a perpetual learning and improving state. It takes on qualities which lead to peak performance such as intuitiveness, spontaneity and instinct. When the mind is in awareness-centered consciousness, unattached to mistakes, peak performance is a natural outcome.

David Freeze

In the 2011 World Series between the Saint Louis Cardinals and the Texas Rangers, game six was a "do or die" experience for the Cardinals, who were behind three games to two. This could have been an elimination game for them. Everything was on the line — win or go home. All the overworked clichés fit the scenario. Mistakes in a game such as this can easily be magnified and blown out of proportion, leading to a team either gaining momentum or collapsing completely.

In the top of the fifth inning, with the Rangers at bat, David Freeze, third baseman for the Cardinals, dropped an easy pop fly. This led to more at bats for the Rangers who were able to score some runs. It was the kind of mistake that could have cost the Cardinals the game. But Freeze was able to accept and mentally let go of his mistake rather than allowing it to become a distraction. He shrugged off the error and seemed to simply take it in stride. For many athletes, such an error could have become a devastating blow to the fragile psyche of the ego. Instead of seeing the mistake as a cause for losing the game and damaging his reputation, Freeze took it as a challenge. He might have become the goat of the World Series, and it seemed likely that because he was a hometown boy pressure would be on him for the rest of the game. The Cardinals were down to their final strike and the last person at bat to get a hit or go home was, of course, David Freeze. He doubled off the right field wall to tie the game. But his best heroics were yet to come. Freeze proceeded to hit a walk-off home run in the bottom of the eleventh inning to win the game and tie the World Series at three games apiece. The topper was that the Cardinals proceeded to win game seven, six to two. David Freeze won the World Series MVP honors.

The Ego Performer on the Mental Pathway

The ego performer on the mental pathway is stuck in the duality of attachment to the positive (caring too much) and withdrawal from the negative (caring too little). She divides attention between forced focus (concentration) and scattered focus. Her attention is divided. One voice says, "Be smart, use your head." Another says, "That was stupid!" Good shot versus bad shot- Forced positive thinking versus negative thinking- Right versus wrong.

The ego sports performer desires the high end, positive thoughts, and resists the low end, negative thoughts, within ego-centered consciousness. By forcing the mind to think positively, the ego *thinks* it can create awareness, when in reality the mind will naturally think positively if the mind is in awareness-centered consciousness. When the ego forces the mind to think positively, it automatically manufactures a resistance to its opposite, negative thinking. Trying to reverse-engineer awareness-centered consciousness through the mind is often referred to as "mental toughness" training. It wants the logical mind to override emotion. This approach to the mental game advocates a forced focus of the mind, or concentrating harder. It seeks to impose on the mind a state of total focus and discipline conditioned through hard work and repetition. Mental toughness training also wants the left side of the brain, the logical side, to override and control negative mental emotional reactive patterns that have been conditioned from early childhood. Phrases such as, "Stay positive," "Just win," "Concentrate," "Dominate your opponent," "Be tough," and "Don't quit," all seem good. They make this method look like it leads to success, but that success is temporary. Ultimately, forced positive thinking manifests a bigger battle than your opponent or the opposing team. It conditions an internal mental battle that the ego performer cannot win. You become your own worst enemy.

The ego performer's mind is at war with itself and the athlete becomes a causality of his own thought processes, which also leads to being distracted, distressed, and discouraged. He inhibits performance due to an internal mental fight between what he desires and resists.

Sugar Ray and the "Hands of Stone"

We've all seen sports performances in which an athlete may have seemed like he quit and just started going through the motions. One of the most famous such stories took place on November 25, 1980 in New Orleans, Louisiana, a fight between two legendary boxers, the slick moving, quick-punching and effortless style of Sugar Ray Leonard, a welter-weight version of Mohammed Ali, versus the great Panama fighter Roberto Duran, nicknamed the "Hands of Stone."

This fight was the second of three fights in which the two engaged. The first took place on June 20, 1980 in Montreal, Canada. Duran's style was to go toe to toe and pound his opponent into submission. He had questioned Sugar Ray's fighting and punching ability. Sugar Ray Leonard decided to fight Duran's style and stand up to the "Hands of Stone." Duran won the first fight in a unanimous decision that Sugar Ray dearly wanted to avenge. The second bout was about to become one of the most infamous fights in boxing history.

Sugar Ray Leonard was determined not to make the same mistake he had made in Montreal. He used his slick speed and movement to out-box Duran, throwing quick jabs and combinations while keeping out of the range of Duran's lethal punches. It was obvious as the fight wore on that Duran was becoming mentally worn out and frustrated. He wanted Sugar Ray to stand still and box him, to "fight like a man!" In the seventh round Sugar Ray started to taunt Duran. In the eighth, Duran started looking as though he had had enough. Finally he turned toward the referee and said, "No-Mas" (no more). The "Hands of Stone" had given up. He had become demoralized and was no longer attached to the result of winning. One of the greatest punchers of any weight class threw in the towel. Later he claimed that he had eaten too much in the morning, developed stomach cramps and was thus unable to continue. But Carlos Eleta, his manager, said Duran always ate that way before a fight and that he did not quit because of stomach cramps. Duran was obviously in resistance to the style of fighting that Sugar Ray brought into the ring and lost interest in competing. This fight hurt Duran's image as the consummate puncher. The two would not fight again for another nine years, at which time Sugar Ray would come out on top again. It appears as if the Duran story was a case of a great boxer attached to winning (high end of the ego) becoming withdrawn (low end of the ego) to the point where he quit.

Lance Armstrong

The mind in ego-centered consciousness can become so conditioned to attachment to success that it will go to any means to achieve its objective, including acts of gamesmanship, cheating, threats, and physical violence. A story that brings to light an athlete's will to win at any cost is illustrated by the remarkable, and now infamous, career of a man some considered to be the greatest cyclist of all time, Lance Armstrong. Armstrong won an unprecedented seven

Tour De France championships, which was a remarkable feat. What makes it even more incredible is that he accomplished it even though he was a cancer survivor. Lance partnered with Nike to create the *Live Strong* foundation, which donates millions of dollars to cancer research. On the surface, this story seemed to represent all that is good about the American dream — a famous athlete using his success to help others. Unfortunately, the bubble burst for Lance Armstrong when he admitted to taking steroids, blood doping, and using other performance-enhancing drugs. Armstrong later confessed that his win-at-all-cost attitude drove him to perhaps one of the greatest cheating scandals and cover-ups in sports history.

Kerrigan / Harding

A story which takes the ego's destructive nature to the point of even harming others is the Nancy Kerrigan, Tanya Harding story. In a conspiracy to make sure Tonya Harding would make the US Olympic Team, there was an attempt to injure her chief rival Nancy Kerrigan. It was an incident that has since been referred to as the "whack heard around the world." Tonya Harding's ex-husband, Jeff Galloly, and her bodyguard, Shawn Eckhardt, allegedly hired Shane Start, a man who was supposed to break Kerrigan's right leg so she would not be able to skate. The US Figure Skating Championships were taking place with the top finishers qualifying for the winter Olympic Games. In a practice session in Detroit, Michigan on January 6, 1994, Start used a collapsible police baton to strike Kerrigan a few inches above her knee, severely bruising her leg and forcing her to withdraw from the National Championships.

Tonya Harding went on to win the US Championships qualifying her for the Olympic Team. Kerrigan, however, was given a special exemption which also qualified her for the Olympic team. So the alleged attempt to knock Kerrigan out of the Olympics turned out to be a failure. Although Harding denied that she took part in planning the attack she later admitted to covering up the incident. The United States Figure Skating Association (USFSA) and the US Olympic Committee indicted proceedings to remove Tonya Harding from the Olympic team.   When Harding threatened a lawsuit, however, they backed off. She was allowed to obtain her place on the team.   In the Lillehammer Olympics, Tonya Harding finished eighth while Nancy Kerrigan, now fully recovered and back in form, placed second. She won a silver medal and barely missed out on the gold.

The event was covered by over 400 members of the press, creating a circus-like environment. As a result of this premeditated assault on Nancy Kerrigan, all of the individuals involved except for Tonya Harding served jail time.   On March 6, 1995, it was Harding's turn to fess up. She pleaded guilty on conspiracy to hinder prosecution of the attackers. Her sentence included three years of probation, 500 hours of community service and $160,000 in fines. As part of her plea bargain she was forced to resign from the USFSA and was stripped of her US National Championship Figure Skating title. In addition, she was barred for life from participating as a skater or a coach in any USFSA event.

Even on the high end of the ego, the mind's attachment to winning can take on a destructive nature because the ego does not concern itself with the best interest of others.

The Authentic Performer on the Mental Pathway

The authentic sports performer on the mental pathway creates a shift to an "empty mind" or observer state, bypassing either attach or repel (the duality domain) of the ego. There is a natural intensity of focus, a non-judgmental awareness resulting in natural positive thinking. The authentic performer's mind dissipates negativity because that is not the mind's natural state. The mind is an open receiver which allows information to be processed objectively.

Natural learning takes place through an action/awareness feedback loop which allows the authentic performer to continually adapt to sports-relevant tasks geared to the game's objectives or stated goals. The observer mode of the mind flows in the present moment and has no resistance to what is happening externally. Free from distractions or external factors, the authentic sports performer's mind remains quiet and calm. In the aware mind of the authentic performer there is no need to train the mind up to mental toughness because the mind is naturally resilient, focused, positive, flexible, adaptive and creative.

The authentic performer executes their craft with an effortless ease, divorced from trying, struggle and over-control. The athlete uses the power of the present and the gift of feel to learn and improve in every moment. The authentic performer is in a state of mind/body/sync which does not need to override the mental emotional reactive patterns. The observer state frees the athlete's mind from past conditioning. The authentic performers has no internal mental dialogue taking place, thereby allowing energy and feel to flow towards peak performance.

Sometimes an athlete can start out with an unattached mind and freedom from internal distractions. The athlete can start out their performance in "the zone." The athlete could play in the zone for the entire duration of the contest or something could happen to disturb their unattached mind. I witnessed one such match at the US Open Tennis Championships on September 5, 1985.

Bill's Experience
John McEnroe

While working in New York I used to love attending the US Open, where the best tennis players in the world had the opportunity to showcase their skills. On a Wednesday night quarter-final match, tennis legend John McEnroe was matched up against one of the most consistent base-liners in the world and a top-ten player, Joakim Nystrom. McEnroe was the clear favorite, but the match could prove to be very competitive. The New York crowd is very tennis-knowledgeable, and often very rowdy and loud.

On this particular night McEnroe, a serve and volley player with great touch and precision to his shot making, was playing at a level that was taking my breath away. "Wow!" was the only thing that came to mind. I was sitting next to some spectators in the crowd who were talking about Nystrom as if he was a second-rate tennis player and had no right to be on the court with McEnroe. They did not realize the creative level of genius they were witnessing and the vast potential of the mind in a peak performance state. McEnroe was literally playing "out of his mind," an expression often used to describe peak performance.

McEnroe, like the world's greatest pool players, was running the table. He was running Nystrom from pillar to post and then, with his gracefulness and touch, moved to the net to finish off the points. Unfortunately something happened before McEnroe could finish off the match in his peak performance state. After winning the first two sets 6-1, 6-0 and surrendering very few points off unforced errors, during the third set McEnroe went ahead 2 games to zero and had a break point to go up 3-0.

Normally when a player is broken twice on serve at the professional level there is very little chance of a comeback, especially against a player of McEnroe's caliber. At break point McEnroe hit a forehand winner down the line which was called good and McEnroe proceeded to sit down for the odd-game changeover. McEnroe has a fiery temper and resistance to the perspective that he is being treated unfairly. He has been known to throw tennis temper tantrums. So when the lines person reversed her call and the chair umpire over-ruled McEnroe's winning forehand and called his shot out, McEnroe blew up, pulling him out of his peak performance state. In the final set McEnroe was not playing at the top of his game. Nystrom started to play better in the third set which made it highly contested. McEnroe eventually pulled it out and won 7 games to 5, but when the ego mind takes over, peak performance is not an option. At the highest skill level there are rare athletes that have been able to transcend ego-centered consciousness and create performance from a higher state of consciousness — empty mind, or observer state.

Bruce Lee

A story of an athlete who seemed to create his performance through awareness-centered consciousness is the remarkable career of karate legend, Bruce Lee. While Lee chose not to participate in karate competitions, he was still regarded by many experts in the field as a master of the martial arts. UFC president Dana White called him "the father of mixed martial arts" because of his flexibility, adaptability, and unpredictability when sparring and fighting. Lee was born in San Francisco November 27, 1940, but moved to Hong Kong where he eventually became a master in karate and the art of Kung Fu. He was a student of all fighting arts and won several boxing championships. He moved to back to San Francisco at eighteen years of age and went to school at the University of Washington.

There he started some Kung Fu classes which became more and more popular. The Chinese Karate and Kung Fu masters frowned upon teaching their secrets to non-Chinese due to the fact that their teachings are rooted in their philosophy of life.

As Bruce Lee continued both his intellectual and physical pursuits of excellence he developed a philosophy that called for less of a structural and traditional approach evident in most karate training. For Lee, the martial arts were his chosen path for self-expression. He likened himself to being like water:

> *When you fight, be formless and shapeless like water.*
> *Now, when you put water into a cup it becomes the cup.*
> *When you pour water into a bottle, it becomes the bottle.*
> *If you put water into a teapot, it becomes the teapot.*
> *Water can flow, creep, drip or crash. Be water my*
> *friend...Let your mind be like water (formless, flow*
> *wherever it needs to flow and be whatever it needs to be).*

Lee developed his own style of fighting called *Jun Fan Gung Fu*. He had no need to massage his ego or prove himself in karate championships, although he did beat some very formidable opponents in exhibitions and challenge matches. While he was slight of build and stature, he was a phenomenal athlete. Chuck Norris, six time World Karate Champion and himself a karate legend, was quoted as saying, "Pound for pound, Lee was the strongest man in the world, and likely would win a karate world championship if he participated."

Bruce Lee was able to do unbelievable physical acts, such as one-handed pushups using only his thumbs and index fingers, and 50 repetitions of one armed pull-ups. He was so quick with his hands that he was able to snatch a dime off a person's open hand and leave a penny in its place before they could close their hand. He kept adapting and evolving his style. He was quoted as saying, "Do not dismiss the classical approach simply as a reaction or you will have created another pattern and trapped yourself there."

As this pertains to the mental pathway, the mind functions optimally when it is open, empty and not conditioned by a certain style of karate or form. Predictability and stylistic tendencies create vulnerability and inevitably leads to defeat.

Bruce Lee eventually called his style *Jeet Kune Do*, or the "way of the intercepting fists." Later he regretted this name, for within any style there are too many restrictions, parameters, or limitations, and he wanted martial arts to exist outside any parameters or limitations. He emphasized what he called "the style of no style," consisting of getting rid of the formalized approach which Lee claimed was inherent in traditional styles. His approach to fighting was to deal with the known (the fighting style of his opponent) through the unknown (which we call awareness-centered consciousness). Throughout his life, he opened karate schools and became a celebrated actor in motion pictures. He died unexpectedly on July 20, 1973, of cerebral edema, at the age of 33.

Lee was a man of extraordinary vision and talent, and his untimely death was a great loss to the world. He realized that the key to excellence in any sport is connected to freedom of the mind, a natural outcome of awareness-centered consciousness. As is often quoted in Zen philosophy, "the mind, like a cup, is only useful when it is empty."

Once mental attachments have been cleared, energy and feel are free to flow towards the emotional pathway. Let's discover together the super energy of performance. Welcome to the power of joy and passion!

Chapter 5
Emotion: Pathway to Joy

Emotion is the fuel that either boosts performance on the positive side or undermines sports performance on the negative side. Emotions are feelings that tend to show up unannounced, and often unexpectedly, while engaging in a sporting activity. In relationship to consciousness, emotions are the energy source through which consciousness is felt. They are the driving power of performance, converting consciousness into feeling.

Emotions can either be experienced through awareness-centered consciousness or ego-centered consciousness.

Ego-Centered Consciousness on the Emotional Pathway

In ego-centered consciousness emotions are programmed as part of the mental emotional reactive patterns. They are the result of the indoctrinated and conditioned aspect of the mind. The roots or origins of these mental emotional reactive patterns are often unknown because they have been buried deeply in the unconscious mind. They, just like thought patterns, become a force of habit in ego-centered consciousness.

In ego-centered consciousness there is a sequence based on thinking, feeling, and reacting. If an athlete experiences a *desired* outcome there is positive emotion and positive reaction. If an athlete experiences a *resisted* outcome there is negative emotion and negative reaction. The athlete blocks emotional energy when experiencing a resisted outcome (losing) and unleashes emotional energy when experiencing a desired outcome (winning). This emotional roller-coaster prevents the athlete from getting into a deeper feeling of flow needed for peak performance.

In ego-centered consciousness, emotions lead to reactions. They can serve as a barometer for how an athlete is thinking. If an athlete is experiencing negative emotions, undoubtedly the thought program is responsible. In ego-centered consciousness, an emotional momentum or an emotional inertia develops because of the duality of the ego. The high and low emotional ends of the ego explain the see-saw effect often observed in sporting events. How often have we seen, in a college football or basketball game, for instance, the momentum of a game shifting to one or the other team because of a single play such as a missed field goal, fumble, or missed free throw? This phenomenon, on the emotional pathway in ego-centered consciousness, plays off of a principle of physics that for every action there is an equal and opposite reaction. The play of emotion becomes attached to outcome. So when one player or team's emotion goes up, there tends to be a corresponding emotional reaction in which the other player or team's emotion goes down. When things are going well for the athlete or team, there can be a feeling of happiness, contentment, encouragement, satisfaction, pride, hope, and excitement. Contrarily, when things are not going well, there can be a feeling of despair, frustration, anger, fear, jealousy, and depression.

The ego itself, on the emotional pathway, wants to become comfortable. So in the latter stages of a sporting event an athlete or team will often tend to relax, paving the way for the opponent or opposing team to mount a comeback. Brad Gilbert, a well-known tennis player, commentator and author, referred to this phenomenon as "wounded bear and happy camper." The athlete or team that is ahead relaxes (happy camper), almost hoping that the other player or team just gives up. This allows the other player or team (wounded bear) to become determined, aggressive and re-energized. Comebacks are very often based on this phenomenon.

It is obvious that negative emotions such as frustration, fear, anger, self-pity, and worry, which arise from ego-centered consciousness, do not lead to a peak performance state.

Awareness-Centered Consciousness on the Emotional Pathway

In awareness-centered consciousness emotions flow freely because they are not part of the conditioned mental emotional reactive patterns.   Negative emotions simply dissipate. Emotions come and go without the athlete getting too high or too low. There is always a sense of emotional balance.

In awareness-centered consciousness, the thought process does not determine the emotional response. The mind is in a neutral state of non-resistance which creates a balanced emotional state and surrendered-action. Regardless of any outcome, the athlete is in a continual state of unblocking and releasing energy and feel, rather than being caught in the duality of positive and negative emotion. The energy of passion is experienced as an inexhaustible emotion. This emotional fuel necessary for peak performance is experienced independently from what is happening externally.

In awareness-centered consciousness the athlete does not get caught up in the endless cycle of ego-emotional momentum and ego-emotional inertia. There is a natural sense of excitement and enthusiasm for the process itself, free from an endless ego cycle of ups and downs. The athlete transcends the constant high and low, positive and negative emotions that are dependent on results.

The emotional state in awareness-centered consciousness might best be described as passion with appreciation. It is based in a deep love for the sport free from external factors. Often, if a player or a team is in awareness-centered consciousness they do not experience emotional let-downs, allowing a comeback by the other player or team. Emotions do not hinder the athlete from finishing the task at hand, such as crossing the finish line, without getting overly excited, tense, or passive. Occasionally an athlete experiences a shift out of the desire resistance cycle of ego-centered consciousness and into awareness-centered consciousness on the emotional pathway leading to a remarkable feat.

Carlton Fisk and Pete Rose

One such story involves the great baseball player Carlton Fisk, a catcher who first gained his fame playing for the Boston Red Sox. One of the most famous images in American sports lore is that of Carlton Fisk standing next to home plate in the bottom of the twelfth inning in game six of the 1976 world series, waving his arms wildly to try to will a ball he had just hit to stay fair of the left-field foul pole. Baseball enthusiasts know how this turned out. Fisk's dramatic home run won the game, forcing a deciding game seven against the Cincinnati Reds. Few, however, know of an incident a few innings earlier that greatly affected Fisk`s emotional state as he stepped up to the plate for that famous at-bat. One of his opponents on the Reds, Pete Rose (who is currently the all-time hits leader in baseball history), had come to the plate while Fisk had taken his stance as catcher. The game was close. Tension filled the air. This was the time in the game when it could have been easy to "choke" out of shear nervousness. Just before Rose stepped into the box, he turned back to Fisk and said, "Isn't this fun?" Rose was reveling in the moment, like a little boy just enjoying a game, and loving the challenge that the moment was presenting.

Unbeknownst to Rose, in this simple comment he was probably setting the stage for Fisk`s later heroics. Fisk later reported that he was taken by surprise by Rose's comments. He suddenly realized what an honor it was to be able to participate in such a great game. He probably experienced an emotional shift into awareness-centered consciousness, and likely somewhere deep inside himself accessed the little boy who just loved to play baseball. When he came up to the plate in the bottom of the twelfth he was not anxious about failing or succeeding. He was simply in the moment, playing the game with full joy and abandon. In that emotional state he performed at his highest level, hitting one of the most famous clutch home runs in baseball history.

The Ego Performer on the Emotional Pathway

The ego performer on the emotional pathway is always on an emotional roller-coaster between opposing emotions, dependent upon whether things are going well or not. Traditional training approaches usually try to make the athlete control their negative emotions which inevitably arise, and to artificially generate the so called "positive" emotions. These are two techniques of the dualistic ego-centered mind. The suppression of undesired emotion and the forced manufacturing of desired emotion create an unavoidable tension. This blocks energy and "feel" that could otherwise be freed up to allow for a more effective performance.

Emotions on the high end of the ego may provide temporary satisfaction for the ego performer, and even help to propel the athlete to a higher level performance. However, because the athlete is driven by external factors, energy and feel is restricted and conditional. So this momentary high is often followed by a crash in which performance deteriorates.   Physical displays of screaming, "Come on", yelling after making a shot, pumping your fist or beating your chest are associated with the high end of ego emotion. But, and (this is a big "but!") "what goes up must come down."

The "Big Three" of the Miami Heat

One such story of a team getting emotionally too high, and celebrating too soon, occurred on June 2, 2011 in game two of the NBA finals.   The two teams involved where the Miami Heat, with their three super-star players, LeBron James, Dwayne Wade and Chris Bosh, and the Dallas Mavericks, a team lead by three veteran players — the ageless Jason Kidd, the seven-foot German, Dirk Nowitzki and the super sub, Jason Terry.

The Miami Heat had gotten off to a slow start in the beginning of the season, but began to hit their stride as they rolled into the playoffs. They kept their momentum during the first round, defeating the Philadelphia 76ers, and then beat a tough Boston Celtics team who were the previous year's NBA finalists. Finally they defeated the young and highly talented Chicago Bulls to reach the finals. They silenced their critics and, at least at first, lived up to their expected hype, which had accompanied them ever since the "Big Three" joined together for the 2011 season. In game one of the finals they continued to roll, beating the Dallas Mavericks 92-84. Mentally and emotionally the Miami Heat looked very confident, as if they might just run away with this series. But an interesting thing happened on the way to the NBA title. In game two the Heat broke out to a 12-point lead in the 4th quarter, with the ball in their possession. When they came down the floor, Dwayne Wade got the ball in the right hand corner, sinking a 3-pointer which put the Heat up 88-73 with just 7:15 left in the game.

It certainly seemed, for all intents and purposes, that the game was over at this point. The Heat had a big lead; they were playing well, and appeared to be "feeling it." After Wade made his three-pointer there was a tremendous display of emotion, with a lot of chest bumping and celebrating by the Miami players, as if the game was over. Emotional momentum however, can be tricky. Often the team or player in the lead becomes comfortable, while the team that trails can become focused, intent on making a final stand. When a team becomes overly emotional, a false "high" produced by the results of the score, it often happens that they experience a momentary, emotional, let-down. The players begin to stand around and become frozen like a deer in headlights. This is exactly what appeared to happen to the Miami Heat in game two.

As the Dallas Mavericks cut away at the Miami lead, the Heat began to lose their teamwork, percentage shot selection, and emotional cool. The Mavericks slowly erased the Miami lead and tied the score 93 with just seconds left. Then Dirk Nowitzki proceeded to hit a last second shot to win the game. It looked as though the Miami Heat's bubble had popped as they snatched defeat out of the jaws of victory. This game appeared to be the pivotal game in the series as Miami mustered enough energy to take game three, which would have given them a virtually insurmountable lead of three games to zero had they won the second game.

We suggest, taking nothing away from Dallas, that the Heat's untimely emotional celebration in game two probably cost them the series. They lost the series to the Mavericks, four games to two. To their credit, however, they seemed to have learned from this untimely emotional celebration. They learned the value of appreciating their performance without emotionally getting too high or too low as they went on to win the NBA title the following two years.

Steffi Graf and Jana Novotna

The ego performer on the emotional pathway can either end up withdrawing emotion (tanking) or overloading on emotion (choking) under stress. Very often this leads to paralysis or an inability to perform. One example of an athlete being on the verge of victory and then letting emotion get the best of her took place during the Wimbledon finals on July 4, 1993, between Steffi Graf and the talented Czech, Jana Novotna. Steffi Graf, known as "Fraulein Forehand," possessed probably the most dominant stroke in the history of women`s tennis. Her hall of fame career includes 22 grand-slam victories. Many experts consider her to be the greatest female tennis player of all time. Jana Novotna was an athletic all-court player, who was capable of beating anyone in the world on any given day. She was more renowned, however, for her inconsistency, and had never won a grand slam title. Some experts at the time considered her the best player never to win a slam.

On this day Novotna had a flawless game plan against Steffi Graf, mixing up her beautiful serve and volley game to Graf's backhand. At other times Novotna stayed on the baseline and waited patiently to attack Graf's backhand, moving to the net to finish the point. Even though Graf was able to win the first set, during the tiebreaker Novotna was playing well and Graf was fortunate to win it.

Novotna breezed through the second set six games to one and was ahead in the third set. Serving for an almost insurmountable lead of 5-1, she attempted a huge second serve but double-faulted, opening the door slightly for Graf. At 4-1, down in the third set, Graf had only won two of the previous ten games. Novotna was clearly out-playing Graf, and probably had she just spun her second serve into the backhand she would have won the match. Graf, however, was able to pick up her energy and began to play better. Novotna began to play with less conviction, and her emotional state seemed to become more and more blocked. She started missing shots which she previously had been making and there seemed to be a look of resignation on her face. She looked emotionally frozen, and the momentum and eventual outcome of the match totally swung in Graf's direction.

When Graf won the last point and approached the net for the traditional handshake, Graf noticed that Novotna looked sick and asked her if she felt okay. In an interview after the match Graf was quoted as saying, "With the way Jana was playing and the way I was playing, I kind of lost it. I did not give up but I did not have a positive feeling."

During the trophy presentation, the Duchess of Kent was quoted as saying to Jana, "Don't worry. I know you can do it". At that point the tears started to flow and everyone could see the emotional pain that Novotna was going through. We suspect that the emotions shown after losing the match had been blocked during the final stages of the third set leading to a kind of emotional paralysis, blocking feel. Jana may have been better served in that third set by getting angry and letting her emotions out rather than holding them back. Novotna, however to her credit did not let this match, which was voted the greatest tennis "choke" of all time by the tennis channel, put an end to her grand-slam chances. She made it to the 1997 Wimbledon finals, losing to Martina Hingis. In her third try, in 1999, she won the Wimbledon title against Nathalie Tauziat. At the age of 29, she became the oldest first-time winner of a grand slam final in the Open era.

The "Bartman Incident"

The effects of negative or positive emotions on consciousness can affect a community and create an environment either conducive to or detrimental to success. One of the most infamous stories where negative emotion deflated a team, as well as an entire community, took place in Chicago. It happened on October 14, 2003, at Wrigley field, during game six of the National League championship game between the Chicago Cubs and the Florida Marlins. At this point in the series the Cubs were ahead three games to two.

Past history has not been kind to the Cubs, (to put it mildly). Their major league drought without winning a championship had at that time spanned nearly 100 years. The Chicago Cubs are often referred to as the "lovable losers." This type of label can carry with it strong negative emotions — the feeling that no matter how close they get to a major league championship, something will go wrong.

In the eighth inning of game six with the Chicago Cubs holding a three-run lead, the baseball gods would once again rain on the Cubs parade. What appeared to be a catchable pop fly down the left field line off the bat of Luis Castillo was drifting toward the stands. Many of the fans put their hands in the air to catch the ball if luck would bring it to them. Trying to catch foul balls is a very common and natural reaction for fans at baseball games, who love to catch a souvenir ball. One of the fans, Stephen Bartman, reached for the ball and deflected it, disrupting a potential catch by outfielder Moises Alou.

Was the foul ball catchable? Alou certainly thought so, and became visibly upset. The entire Chicago team, which was riding the momentum of positive emotion, seemed to become totally deflated. If Alou had caught the ball the Cubs would have two outs in the inning and be just four outs away from winning the pennant and going to the World Series, possibly getting a huge gorilla off their backs.

As we said earlier, when one team tends to become emotionally negative the other team's emotions tend to go up, becoming positive. The Florida Marlins ended up scoring eight runs in that inning and eventually won the game. Bartman was escorted out of Wrigley field and placed into police custody for fear that the emotional fans might take their loss out on him. In ego-centered consciousness, when emotions become negative there is a tendency to lash out and look for blame. There was still another game to play, however, between the Cubs and the Marlins.

In game seven, when the Cubs fans needed to be in a celebratory mood with the excitement about the possibility of going to the World Series, there was a kind of resignation in the stadium, a feeling that the Cubs were doomed to lose. This feeling seemed to be present both with the fans and the team itself. The Florida Marlins went on to win game seven, and subsequently the 2003 World Series. We suggest that the collective consciousness of negative emotions, not only from the players but also from the fans, were at the root of the Cub's collapse in game six.

The Authentic Performer on the Emotional Pathway

The authentic performer on the emotional pathway experiences sports through the "observe" mode of consciousness. In this non-dualistic state there is no conflict because non-resistance creates only appreciation and gratitude, which are not connected to external factors. Emotions are not attached to whether things are going well or not. The authentic performer's emotions transcend the known and rise up from the unknown, dissipating negative emotions. They are connected to higher emotional states of love and joy. Emotions that are dependent upon external factors (the known) are just as likely to bring you down as pump you up.

The authentic performer allows emotions to flow freely, without judging them. They are like clouds, coming and going. The authentic performer always does his or her best. Passion is not based on ego desires, resistance, or positive and negative emotion, but rather on a deep love for the game without any attachment to a particular result. The way to access this state or feeling is not to try and generate a positive feeling, but rather by effortlessly letting go of emotion. You simply notice emotions as they arise. By not attaching to them they won't take hold of the mind. This allows ego-based emotion to lose its energy and dissipate. The releasing of emotional energy as it is occurring actually sets free more energy and feel that naturally resides in awareness-centered consciousness. This is a freeing feeling of great passion just to play without holding anything back while experiencing a deep appreciation and gratitude for the opportunity to do so.

Jennifer Rodriquez

A story which illustrates how love, gratitude, and appreciation can reignite an athlete's passion to continue playing a sport is the story of speed skater Jennifer Rodriquez. Rodriquez is a Cuban American speed skater from Miami. Her path to becoming a speed skater and earning the nickname "Miami Ice" started when she was an artistic roller skater. She won multiple national championships and placed second and third in the world championships. She later switched sports to in-line skating, where she also achieved great success by becoming the world champion in 1993. Probably to challenge herself, and possibly have a chance to compete in the Olympics, Rodriquez took up speed skating. She made multiple Olympic teams and competed in the 1998 Nagano, Japan, the 2002 Salt Lake City, the 2006 Turin, Italy, and the 2010 Vancouver, Canada winter Olympics.

Rodriquez had many emotional challenges over the course of her long career as a speed skater. She went through a difficult divorce, suffered financial problems, and experienced the death of her mother in 2009, the woman Rodriquez acknowledged as her greatest fan. While she did not win the gold medal at the Olympics, she did win two bronze medals in the 2002 Salt Lake City games.

Her speed skating career almost came to an abrupt end in 2006, when she decided to hang up her skates. This was possibly due to the years of training and endless hours of practice. The amount of desire and energy it takes to compete at the highest level can easily lead to burnout. Something happened, however, that would rekindle her passion for the sport and unlock the emotions needed to continue her career. In 2008, after being off her skates for two years, she was asked by her husband at the time to help work with some children at the Miami Skating Club. She agreed to help, and when she went out on the ice for the first time in two years an outpouring of emotion overcame her. She cried simply because she loved her sport. It was at that point she realized that she had stopped skating too soon.

This release of emotional tension led to a re-commitment to continue her speed-skating career. She began to work for a place on the team that would compete in the 2010 Olympic games in Vancouver, Canada.

On faith, and without a lot of money, she moved to Park City, Utah, where the US national speed skating team trains year round. Rodriquez is quoted as saying, "Definitely I am having a lot more fun with skating. I am really enjoying myself and I look forward to practice every day, where before [I went] to practice because [I] had to." She renewed herself and her passion, finding again the joy of skating. Even her mother's death in 2009 due to breast cancer did not become a reason for her to stop training. She realized that her mom would have wanted her to continue and it is likely that death became a source of inspiration rather than a source of discouragement.

While Rodriquez did not win a medal in the 2010 winter Olympics, her story illustrates the fact that when you love a sport and are able to release blocked emotions, the natural feeling of appreciation, passion and gratitude shows up.

Magic Johnson

The authentic performer on the emotional pathway naturally exhibits a love, passion and joy for the game that is noticeable to everyone watching. One player that exhibited all those traits was the Hall of Fame and former Los Angeles Laker's point guard, Earvin (Magic) Johnson.

Johnson started his publicized basketball career in his sophomore year in high school while playing point guard for Lansing Everett High

School in Michigan. It was during a high school game in which he recorded a "triple double" of 36 points, 18 rebounds and 16 assists, that he was given the name by which he would become famous. The game was being covered by Fred Stabley Jr., a writer for the Lansing State Journal. Because of his unbelievable performance Stabley coined the nickname "Magic".

Throughout Magic's college and professional careers, he competed with a smile on his face and an enthusiasm for the game which was contiguous to even the seasoned professionals who played with him. He was a consummate leader who made everyone around him better, and had such a feel for the game that he seemed to have eyes in the back of his head. Fans, as well as NBA players, loved watching Magic play. The joy he brought to the game is one of his many lasting legacies. When passion and joy become emotional fuel, peak performance is a natural outcome.

The next place energy and feel can be blocked is the relationship pathway. Let's discover together the true essence of relationships. Welcome to the power of oneness!

Chapter 6
Relationship: Path to Wholeness

Relationships are the fabric of life itself. They represent everything that is not me, you, we, or us. They are the world of the "other," all things that are outside of who we think we are. In sports, relationships set up opposition that lends itself to competition such as "you versus me" and "us against them." Relationships become a measuring stick for sports performance that determines winners and losers.

Ego-Centered Consciousness on the Relationship Pathway

Relationships in ego-centered consciousness produce a struggle for supremacy with the inherent tension manufactured by "me versus you" or "us versus them." This fight to be superior generates a conflict and tension that interferes with peak performance. Relationships become based in survival instincts of fight or flight, dominance and submission and survival of the fittest. In this realm, the player or players with the greater ego-strength will typically prevail, as long as the skill between the opponents is comparable.

Most coaches and athletes in our culture focus on how to win the battle against the opponent in the realm of ego-centered consciousness. They condition a viewpoint of polarized opposites in order to strengthen a sense of an antagonistic enemy that is in a contest for supremacy. Strategies within this approach tend to only be relatively successful. Strategies such as exposing weaknesses, "divide and conquer", and breaking down the will of the opponent are drilled into a players mind. These war-based strategies are grounded in survival instincts of dominance and submission. This desire for dominance and resistance to submission never leads to peak performance.

Awareness-Centered Consciousness on the Relationship Pathway

Relationships, in awareness-centered consciousness, create a spirit of unity and cooperation. There is a natural focus on each player or team moving toward their greatest potential, regardless of who wins or loses. Relationships reside in a non-dualistic state. Rather than conflict there exists a harmony between opposites (opponents). An athlete can experience this non-dualistic harmonious state with their opponent even if the opponent, team members, or other team are in a state of conflict or ego-centered consciousness. This higher state can be present each moment, unaffected by others egos.

Rather than a battle between "you versus an opponent" or a team versus another team, there is a higher, more unified state, which is referred to as "paradoxical unity." In this state, all participants feel as if they are on a mission together. They realize that "if you do your best and I do my best," the performance as a whole will be greater. Conventional thought would view this principle as counter-intuitive, a sabotaging of your own performance by wishing well for your opponent. Contrary to popular belief, however, feeling united with your opponent, in an athletic endeavor, raises your consciousness and leads to peak performance.

In awareness-centered consciousness all relationships work for you regardless of your opponent's resistance. The feeling of connection versus the feeling of separation releases the tension of duality, which allows for action based on the whole. Contrary to traditional sports logic the whole includes all participants in a competitive endeavor. It is inclusive rather than exclusive. There is no enemy or threat and there is no feeling of separation between "for" and "against." When action is based on the whole, you experience what Buddhist philosophy calls "spontaneous right action." Right action is action based on the whole allowing for creativity, intuition, and observation. Spontaneous right action does not occur when there is a separation or resistance between you and your opponent or even you and the crowd.

Federer versus Djokovic

One event that demonstrates an athlete's ability to go beyond the ego on the relationship pathway and tap into awareness-centered consciousness took place at the US Open tennis championships in 2011. The semi-final match between Roger Federer, who some call "the goat" or the greatest of all time, and Novak Djokovic, who is affectionately known as "the joker." At that time Novak was the #1 ranked player in the world.

The crowd was clearly for Roger Federer, the veteran, entering the twilight of his career and the possessor of 17 grand slam titles. The match had been going on for over three and half hours. Federer won the first two sets 7-6, 6-4, and Djokovic won the next two sets 6-3, 6-2. In the fifth and deciding set, Federer elevated his game. His brilliant shot making ability allowed him to take a 5-3, 40-15 double-match point lead. At this point all the momentum and crowd energy was with him, and it seemed that with just one more serve the match would be over. As Djokovic went over to receive serve, the crowd was feverishly cheering on Federer.

Djokovic, with a feeling of acceptance, lifted up his hands and shrugged his shoulders as if to say, "I don't mind that you're for Roger Federer. Whatever happens will happen. I accept the outcome." At that point, what John McEnroe called "one of the greatest shots of all-time" was about to transpire. Federer played an out-wide serve to Djokovic`s forehand. Without any hesitation Djokovic hit a forehand cross-court winner that looked like it went back faster than the original serve. There was a sense, even though Federer had another match point that this incredible shot was worth more than one point. It had an impact on the consciousness of the whole stadium. The crowd stood up and started cheering for Djokovic. Djokovic seemed to find greater energy and resolve and was able to raise his game to a higher level. He rattled off the next four games of the match and won it 7-5 in the fifth. Federer was quoted as saying that Djokovic, before that incredible shot, was "mentally out of it," and he described the shot as desperate. He said it was "just one lucky shot at the end and off you go."

We believe that when Djokovic shrugged his shoulders he became unattached to the outcome of the match.   He let go of any resentment or resistance he might have had towards the crowd being against him, which enabled him to relax and take a risk — what many thought was just a lucky shot.   We believe that when he released his tension about the crowd he was able to access awareness-centered consciousness with its corresponding greater feel, which enabled him to play at a higher level. This was no accident. Djokovic went on to have one of the greatest years in the open era, winning three out of the four grand slam titles, the US

Open, Wimbledon, and the Australian. He also won a record five master series titles just below the importance of the grand slams and accumulated a match record of 70 and 6, including helping his country of Serbia win the Davis Cup, the international team championships.

The Ego Performer on the Relationship Pathway

The ego performer on the relationship pathway is stuck in the program of "for and against." The ego performer is for himself or his team and is against his opponent or the other team.   Coaches tend to motivate their players to have a greater sense of for and against. Sports sayings, such as "this is our house," "dominate the opposition," "let's go out and take it" or "have the heart of a champion" are all ways of moving players to the high end of the ego. For every force, however, there is an equal and opposite counter force. The opposing player or team is operating from the same artificial or man-made duality or animal survival consciousness. This consciousness of both player and team operating from "for and against" manufactures a confrontational approach to sports, so the player or the team with the stronger sense of "for" themselves and "against" the other will generally win. This inherent separation creates a tension that will only lead to drama, suffering, struggle, conflict, tension, and trying too hard.

 The ego performer on the relationship pathway operates in a negative way against the opponent and often with their own team and even themselves. Trash talking, placing blame, making excuses, criticizing, selfishness, rationalization, rejection and intolerance are all tools of the ego performer. These are tools used to build up or enhance yourself or your team and break down the opponent or opposing team.

The "for and against" approach not only goes against the other person or team but can also affect the ego performer's own team. How many times have you watched a game on television in which a player becomes disruptive to team chemistry? A player can be so much for himself that he hurts his team. This "for and against" programming is so conditioned in the world of sports that when a player is unable to manufacture a strong desire for himself and against the opponent it leads to lackluster performances.

Serena and Venus Williams

Nowhere is this more evident than what can be seen in the rivalry between the Williams sisters, Serena and Venus. They played 23 times between 1998 and 2012, with Serena winning 13 times and Venus 10.

The sisters lived their early childhood in a tough neighborhood in Compton, California, where their very survival was threatened. Tennis became their way out. It seems reasonable to assume that these two exceptional athletes conditioned a strong sense of "for us" and "against others," which led to a strong desire to excel and their remarkable success on the pro tour. To date they have won a combined 23 Grand Slam singles titles between them. But for those who watched them play each other, the quality of many of their matches was disappointing considering the potential of that particular match-up of super stars. Many of their matches did not bring out the flair and aggressiveness that was the trademark of their game. Some of their rallies became hit-or-miss affairs marked by unforced errors, inconsistent play and lack of emotional fire and energy. It did not appear that they were able to reach their top form against each other.

We propose that the Williams sisters found themselves in a "lose-lose" situation. They really did not want to play each other, beat each other, or lose to each other. They were very close as sisters, and one sister's success would take away from the other. They were both identified, in essence, with family success, with both sisters doing well. They were, therefore, unable to perform their best tennis against each other. It was as if they were playing themselves. Without a strong sense of "for and against," the ego performer has difficulty generating the energy it takes for a high level of performance.

There is a direct correlation between the greatest champions and the greatest egos. When a person or team reaches a position in which others feel they are the heavy favorite, there is a tendency to overestimate and award too much credit. This conditioning towards the high end of the ego leads to a sense of pecking order, "rank-ism," and a sense of superiority or inferiority. In the realm of the ego performer, admission of inferiority becomes a self-fulfilling prophecy. There have been many players and teams that garnered so much respect from their opponent that the outcome seemed inevitable. This was the case recently seen in the great Chicago Bulls team of the 90s lead by superstar Michael Jordan. Another player who received so much praise, respect and admiration is the great golfer Tiger Woods. When players or teams are hyped with labels such as "great," "the best," and "dominant," they take on a persona. They can be viewed as almost nonhuman, beyond the reach of ordinary individuals —a kind of superman or woman, a super squad possessing extra powers. One such title was given to the legendary race car driver, Dale Earnhardt.

The "Intimidator"

Earnhardt has been regarded by many as the greatest NASCAR driver of all time. He was known for his aggressive driving style and his "win at any cost" driving tactics, leading a few competitors to accuse him of what many considered to be dirty driving tactics, such as bumping cars out of his way if it would give him track advantage. The threat of seeing the one called "The Intimidator" in the rear-view mirror made many drivers afraid and nervous of being bumped into a crash.

Dale Earnhardt was able to win 76 races and seven Sprint Cup championships. The seven championships tied him with "The King," Richard Petty for the most in Nascar history. They were not a result of him wrecking cars, but rather a result of his phenomenal driving skills, along with his desire to do anything to win. This earned him tremendous respect from his fellow drivers and their teams, a fact made evident in the 1998 Daytona 500 when, after 18 years of frustration and bad luck, he finally won the big title that had eluded him. At the finish of the race every team came out to shake Dale Earnhardt's hand as he drove around the infield.

Unfortunately, Dale Earnhardt lost his life in the same race he most coveted, the 2000 Daytona 500. The racing community still mourns the loss of this great champion. His strong personality and aggressive driving style displayed a strong "for and against" conditioning which allowed him to perform at the high end of the ego on the relationship pathway. The sporting world, and the world in general, operates through the ego on the relationship pathway in which people are only valued for how good they are within their chosen sport or work.

The Authentic Performer on the Relationship Pathway

Authentic performers are free from the program of "for" and "against." They embrace their opponent as part of a shared experience. They need no outside motivation because they feel a natural, instinctive feel to grow, learn, and get better through relationships. The authentic performer recognizes that without the opponent or other team, no growth or learning is possible. In fact, when you wish the best for your opponent, you are enhancing your own ability to play at a high level. This spiritual principle — what you give to others you give to yourself — is naturally present in the authentic performer.

The authentic sports performer expands their feel and consciousness to include the other players or team. This holistic consciousness is a byproduct of moving out of the program of "for" and "against" by accessing their natural observation state. This state is naturally inclusive and free of judgment and duality, even if the opposing player or team is antagonistic, reflecting the negativity of the ego performer. Rather than producing an equal and opposite counter force, the authentic performer taps into the power of the whole, despite any divisive tactics of other players or teams.

Authentic performers are not in resistance to anything the opposition does. This is similar to a principal in martial arts. When the opponent pushes, you pull, and when the opponent pulls, you push. The opponent, in essence, is using their own force against themselves. This creates a greater flow and non-confrontational approach, an approach that leads to surrendered actions, joy, effortless effort, relaxation, and allowing for whatever is called for.

Authentic performers, in embracing the other team and themselves as a single entity, allow negativity to drop away, creating a positive state that is only possible when negativity does not exist. Complimenting, responsibility, accountability, non-judgment, selflessness, harmonious, being with what is, acceptance and tolerance are all natural by-products of the authentic performer on the relationship pathway. These natural feelings elevate the performance of those participants to a higher state of consciousness.

Navratilova / Evert

"Seeking together" is the original spirit of competition. Occasionally, in the world of sports, two players or teams are so closely matched that a rivalry is created based more on mutual respect than on dominance and submission. Players' moving to a state of mutual respect neutralizes the ego, allowing the contestants to bring out their greatest potential. Never was this more evident than what could be considered one of the greatest rivalries in sports history between Martina Navratilova and Chris Evert. They played an amazing 80 times between 1973 and 1988, a 15-year rivalry that left Navratilova holding a slight edge of 43 to 37. They played an amazing 61 finals, with Navratilova winning 36 times and Evert 25 times. They met in 14 Grand Slam finals, with Navratilova holding a 10 to 4 edge.

Chris Evert won 157 titles in her career. Her match record was 1,309 wins to 145 losses, which is a winning percentage of 90.5%, a winning percentage that is the greatest in tennis history. Navratilova was equally impressive, winning 167 titles with a match record of 1,142 wins and 219 losses and a winning percentage of 86.8%. These two great champions were a contrast in both style and temperament. Chris, affectionately known as "the ice maiden," epitomized focus, consistency, and a brilliant tennis IQ. Martina was a phenomenal athlete, a great all-court player with good hands and an amazing touch at the net. She had a fierier temperament, and wore her emotions on her sleeve.

Navratilova defected from Czechoslovakia and became a US citizen in order to enhance her tennis career. Early on in their rivalry, she and Evert were friends and practice partners. They even won two Grand Slam doubles titles together in 1975 and 1976. In the first half of their rivalry, 1973 through 1979, Evert dominated with a 25 to 9 winning record. In 1980 Martina started a physical fitness regime orchestrated by the great "red shark" of women's basketball, Nancy Lieberman. Lieberman felt that Navratilova had too much respect for Evert and that she needed to cultivate more hostility.

While this is really not the spirit of "seeking together," this splitting of the ways may have helped Navratilova get more on the high end of the ego. But it ultimately did not take away from their friendship or the mutual respect they had for each other which help transcend the ego of "for" and "against."

From 1979-1988 the rivalry shifted to Navratilova's favor. Martina won 34 matches to 12. Chris Evert stated that the bond between the two grew over this incredible 15 year rivalry even when Navratilova was winning more head-to-head matches. Evert sought to make herself a better athlete by focusing on getting in better physical shape while working on her nutrition. We believe Evert made Navratilova better and Navratilova made Evert better. There was reciprocity in their relationship that overrode their personal egos of "for" and "against."

It can be observed, and seems abundantly clear, that when you play a sport with passion and love, and when you play for something greater than yourself, all competitors and team members benefit and play at a higher level. This can be seen in many instances in sports and was made very evident by the great point guard Steve Nash, who was so connected to his teammates that he elevated everyone's level of play.

A team playing as one is the essence of team play. There is no "I" in team, and to the degree members of a team can embrace selflessness will greatly determine the team's performance and its ability to rise to its highest potential. Assisting, giving and sharing are attributes of higher consciousness, moving the athlete towards peak performance on the relationship pathway.

Japan Soccer

In July 2011, at the FIFA world cup soccer finals between the USA and Japan, we witnessed the pinnacle of consciousness on the relationship pathway. Japan was a country that was not noted for its soccer accomplishments. On March 11, 2011, a major earthquake struck Japan, triggering a tsunami which eventually caused a nuclear meltdown. Over 20,000 people were reported dead or missing as the result of the tsunami. The physical, mental, and emotional toll that this disaster caused is almost unfathomable. Japan's women's soccer team offered the country a ray of hope in the midst of this tragedy and despair. They had never won a world cup title or major championship, but they were about to do the impossible while becoming a team of destiny.

Japan's coach, Norio Sasaki, motivated his team not through a "for" or "against" approach but rather by showing them photographs of the devastation on Japan's northeast coast, where many homes and people were washed away by the tsunami. To make things even more memorable, Japan had to get through 3 powerhouse women's soccer teams to win the world cup. In the Quarterfinals, the

Japanese team was able to defeat the #2 world-ranked German team 1-0. In the semifinals, they beat a powerful Sweden team 3-1. In the finals they had the daunting task of beating the #1 ranked team in the world- the USA team.

The USA team was led by the great forward Abby Wambach and goalie Hope Solo. It certainly seemed that playing against the powerful US team, the Japanese Cinderella story would come to an end. But trailing 2-1 late in the game, they were able to score the tying goal. With neither team scoring in overtime, the game would come down to penalty kicks. There the Japanese won the game 3-1, winning the World Cup title.

We feel that Japan's improbable run to the World Cup championship transcended ego and raised consciousness by demonstrating the power in playing for a cause greater than an individual or team. This valiant group of Japanese woman played for a country in mourning.

When consciousness expands to include the greater whole, the level of individual and group performance is also raised. Once the energy has expanded beyond "for" and "against," the next place energy and feel can be blocked is the physical pathway. Let's discover the infinite intelligence of your body's wisdom. Welcome to the power of your personal vehicle for peak performance!

Chapter 7
Physical: Pathway to Peak Performance

The physical pathway encompasses the world we see of forms, including the physical body and the environment that surrounds us. In sports, the physical pathway includes the athletic performance, game, and stage it is played on. It is the athlete performing in a pool or on a field, court, course, track and so on. An athlete's sports performance is an effect or what shows up based on talent, skill set, training and consciousness. In relationship to consciousness, an athlete's performance can either be experienced in ego-centered consciousness or awareness centered consciousness.

Ego-Centered Consciousness on the Physical Pathway

In ego-centered consciousness an athlete's physical performance takes on a mechanical programming or conditioning. The mind and body are viewed as separate entities. Consciousness is discounted as the primary cause for peak performance. So there is an emphasis on conditioning the body, mastering a skill set form and strategy in order to reach peak performance. Ego-centered consciousness programs a separation between mind and body, and body and environment, the totality of everything that surrounds the body.

105

There is a sense that the body is pitted against the environment and that it must somehow conquer it. This is the mentality of survival of the fittest — the strong will survive and the weak will perish. Training the body becomes the primary conquest. "Bigger, stronger, and faster" is the ego's battle cry. The body is treated like a machine, to program or fix through repetition. Habits of replicating a certain form and execution are driven to become automatic so there will be no breakdowns in the athletic performance.

Awareness-Centered Consciousness on the Physical Pathway

In awareness-centered consciousness, the physical acts as an extension of consciousness itself. Consciousness is integrated to include everything in the physical world. The mind and body are unified in a natural feel state with an emphasis on feeling the body and environment while allowing the body's wisdom to expand and evolve.

In order for there to be peak performance, an aware mind and aware body are accessed. This is your natural "feel" state. When conscious control of the body is surrendered there is no longer an experience of conflict or separation from the environment. In awareness-centered consciousness you feel a sense of harmony with the environment. Your body becomes a vehicle of "feel," and expresses performance based on that quality. The more "feel" connection between body and environment, the greater the performance. Rather than training the body to overcome the environment, the athlete's consciousness seeks balance with the environment by creating a holistic, integrated response through the body's sense of feel. The body moves to a state of non-resistance. It is relaxed, and at ease. Physically, there is a natural sense of rhythm, timing and feel, in which all actions flow perfectly.

To surrender the body's actions requires embracing the unknown and letting go of trying to control your body and outer circumstances. When an athlete is able to embrace the unknown and surrender his actions, peak performance happens.

Michael Jordon

On June 3, 1992, in game one of the NBA finals between the Portland Trail Blazers and the Chicago Bulls, the Bulls were led by their legendary superstar Michael Jordan. In the first half of this memorable game, Jordan scored 35 points and buried six three pointers, setting an NBA record. The record of 33 points was previously held by Hall of Famer and legendary L.A. Laker Elgin Baylor. After making his sixth three-pointer of the half, Michael Jordan turned towards the broadcast booth, held his arms up in the air, and shrugged his shoulders. That famous shrug, which became a highlight reel mainstay in the sport's world, indicated that Jordan was surprised by his own actions. He was clearly in the peak performance state referred to as "the zone." This only happens when an athlete is unattached to the result and has no resistance to the physical environment. Jordan shrugging his shoulders indicated that his performance was not something that he was in control of. Even the greatest athletes reach this state only on rare occasions.

Peak performance is a direct by-product of a higher conscious state which cannot be captured, trained for, or controlled. Only through the absence of trying to physically control what is going on while tapping into a holistic feeling state is peak performance possible.

The Ego Performer on the Physical Pathway

The ego performer is wrapped up in physically controlling and overcoming outer circumstances. Strength is desired and weakness is resisted. The tension between these polar opposites conditions a sense of trying to acquire strength while opposing weakness. The effort and struggle of trying to be strong while resisting being weak stores tension on the physical pathway. Very often the ego performer fails to listen to his/her body wisdom in an effort to be bigger, stronger, and faster. An inherent struggle prevails in which the ego performer can never seem to be strong enough to completely dominate and conquer any physical obstacles in his/her path. This compulsive desire to be stronger can lead to looking for shortcuts to improve physical strength, stamina, and speed, such as the use of steroids or performance enhancing drugs. This desire for the high end of physical strength can lead, ironically, to its opposite — physical weakness. Weakness is simply the other side of the coin of conflicting opposites on the physical pathway. Whenever there is a desire for strength, weakness will show up.

The quest to find an edge in order to be strong, to dominate the opposition, can ultimately lead to weakness and self-destruction. It is clearly evident in the abuse of steroids and performance enhancing drugs. One story about how the quest for strength and the resistance to weakness can lead to self-destruction is the tragic story of Lyle Alzado.

Lyle Alzado

Lyle Alzado played 15 seasons in the National Football League for the Denver Broncos, Cleveland Browns, and finally Oakland Raiders, with whom he won Super Bowl XVIII. Alzado was a defensive end known for his intense, aggressive, and intimidating style of play. This 6 foot 3, 254 pound specimen of a man, who terrorized players on the football field, died prematurely at the age of 42 of brain cancer. During his last days Alzado admitted to using anabolic steroids and believed it was the steroids that led to his fatal illness. He said that he began using steroids in 1969 and became addicted to the way it made his body feel. His added strength and muscle gave him a decided advantage on the football field. Alzado said that steroids made him play better on the field, although off the field he did things that only crazy people would do.

He believed, back in the 1970s, that most football players were on steroids. He went from a man who epitomized strength to the other end of the ego coin — a man who epitomized weakness. Near the end of his life he lost his hair and his weight and had to hold on to somebody to walk. He experienced memory loss. His last wish was that no one else would die that way. At what length will the ego go to gain strength, superiority, and dominance?

The ego performer, in the pursuit for more, often experiences repeated overuse of the body. Physical Conditions such as tendonitis or joint problems have shortened many players' careers. Over-physical training has led to burnout and death on the field from heat exhaustion. Even for the numbers of professional athletes who have survived, the effects of over-training and playing while injured has affected the quality of their life after their sport. This is evidenced by the lawsuits by the NFL Players Association versus the NFL on the subject of players not being properly informed on the dangers of concussions.

Ego-conditioned ideas such as "play through the pain," "don't be a wimp," and "mind over matter," have pushed the physical body beyond healthy limits. The body, forced to be in conflict with the mind, others, and environment, will eventually break down and not be able to go on. A story that illustrates this point took place during the Iron Man Triathlon in Hawaii.

Julie Moss

The Iron-Man Triathlon is the ultimate competition between body and nature. Great endurance and stamina is a must in order to be able to swim 2.4 miles, bike 112 miles and run a marathon of 26 miles. To complete even one of these feats would be a great accomplishment. The iron-man requires phenomenal fitness training and is the ultimate test of an athlete's physical endurance limits.

Unexpectedly, Julie Moss, a college student from California, was leading the 1982 women's field late in the race. She had outdistanced the favorite, Kathryn Mccarthy, and had only a mile left to the finish line. As she drew closer her body began to give out. She started collapsing. Her body was telling her "no more." But Julie used her strong will to keep pushing herself towards the finish line, all the while collapsing, then getting up, then walking, then running, and then collapsing, over and over again. She was in a fight between her mind, will, and body. Suddenly her worst fears were realized, as Kathryn McCarthy ran past her with about 30 yards left in the race. Julie was physically exhausted and worn out. She had experienced what runners call "hitting the wall." Julie had to crawl to the finish line. The 1982 Iron Man Competition was being covered by ABC`s wide world of sports. No mass TV audience had ever seen anything like what Julie Moss was suffering through in a sporting event. She took the Iron Man to a whole new audience and changed the face of that competition.

The overcoming of the challenges of the body and nature is often viewed as the pinnacle of physical achievement in sports. You can observe this in extreme athletes, who push the limits of life and death. When athletes become addicted to physical risk and accomplishment, it can have dire consequences. What is often confused with courage is really the high end of the ego and a conditioned risk-taking addiction.   This risk-taking addiction, however, can lead to extraordinary physical achievements.

The Flying Wallandas

Consider, for instance, the story of Karl Wallanda, founder of the *Flying Wallandas*, an internationally known daredevil circus act.

The Wallanda family was most known for performing death-defying high wire acts, often without a net. While many might not associate circus acts with athletic endeavor, the balance, timing, relaxation, focus, strength and fitness — all the requirements of a great athlete — must be performed at an extraordinary level. The Wallendas gained most notoriety for a four-person pyramid on top of cycles on a high wire. In 1928, the Wallandas became associated with the world famous Barnum and Bailey circus. In 1947, the Wallandas developed a three-tiered, seven-person pyramid on a high wire. With excessive risk there is also the potential for disaster, however, and that was exactly what happened during a fatal accident in which several family members died. Risk-taking was apparently in the family genes of the Wallandas because despite this fatal tragedy they continued with their craft.

In 1964, at the incredible age of 69, Karl Wallanda broke a sky-walking distance record of 1800 feet at Kings Island amusement park in Mason, Ohio. This amazing record stood for 39 years until 2008, when Wallanda's grandson, Rick, performed a 2000 foot skywalk at the same place. In 1978, at the age of 73, Karl Wallanda apparently still had a desire for grand accomplishments. He attempted a sky-walk between two buildings at the Coronado plaza in San Juan, Puerto Rico. The high wire was suspended 121 feet above the concrete ground without a safety net. Karl tragically fell to his death when wind speeds exceeded 30 miles an hour. No matter what degree of physical training or expertise, an athlete's temptation for the ego to always push the physical envelope can turn risk taking into destruction and strength into weakness.

Many sports challenge the strength of the physical pathway through risk of severe injury or even death. These include sports like football, mountain climbing, the Iditarod (long distance dog sledding race in brutal conditions in Alaska), boxing and perhaps the epitome of physical abuse and punishment, the UFC or ultimate fighting competition. UFC pits opponents of different fighting styles such as wrestling, boxing, judo, jujitsu and karate against each other.

Throughout history, people have admired a gladiator mentality expressed in mottoes such as "battle to the death" and "only the strong will survive." Athletes on the high end of the ego want to prove that they are the toughest and strongest people on the planet. Despite the possibility of pain, physical abuse, being bloodied, breaking a limb and possibly losing their life, this warring image is often idealized.

Shamrock / Diaz

One display of the high end of the ego on the physical pathway took place in a UFC fight on April 11, 2009 at the HP pavilion in San Jose California. The fight, between Frank Shamrock and Nick Diaz, was stopped at the 3:57 mark of the second round. Diaz, the younger fighter of the two was punching Shamrock senseless. Despite being pummeled and beaten Shamrock would not tap out or throw in the towel. Probably his thinking and motivation was that quitting or giving up might be viewed as a sign of weakness, the ultimate humiliation for a UFC fighter. Surrendering does not fit in with the gladiator code, in which it is somehow noble to fight to the end. With Shamrock bloodied and on the canvas unable to get up, Diaz lifted him up as if to show a great respect for Shamrock and honor him for upholding the gladiator code.

The Authentic Performer on the Physical Pathway

For the authentic performer, body control is a poor substitution for body awareness. For the authentic performer on the physical pathway, duality, or opposing forces of strength versus weakness, is transcended by awareness-centered consciousness, the natural observation "feel" state. For the aware performer the body is a vehicle of consciousness, which allows the body's wisdom to reveal the most balanced, efficient, and effective way to train. All physical training in awareness-centered consciousness is holistic and natural. The mind and body perform as a single entity. There is no inherent conflict between the body and not being strong enough to meet the demands of the sport and opponent.

The authentic performer is in harmony with the body and the conditions of contest, as well as with the opponent. All aspects of the competition are embraced. There is a natural connection between the athlete and all physical challenges. The process of physically being aware of the body as a vehicle for feel expands and unifies all experiences, which eliminates physical opposition between the one who experiences and the experience itself. In this state there is a sense of watching your body perform physical actions with a natural rhythm and timing that is greater than any conditioned reaction.

When there is no duality or opposing force between strength and weakness, the body remains relaxed and in "feel," able to perform on a higher level. The authentic performer's body continually adapts and creates balance for the physical requirements of the sport. Sometimes an athlete is able to neutralize the weakness of the physical body by embracing a physical challenge and accepting the weakness and fragility of the body.

A Very "Special" Olympics

Most people view peak performance as a state only available to the most physically trained and talented athletes, but this story took place at the International Special Olympic games held at the University of Notre Dame in the summer of 1987.   Because of his disability, Cerebral Palsy, a male participant in the gymnastics competition in a wheel chair was brought out on the floor by his coach. He was helped to a standing position. It soon became evident that his goal was to stand on one leg and balance himself. Recognizing the almost impossible task at hand, the crowd waited with breathless anticipation to see what would happen. After several attempts to achieve this remarkable feat the crowd could feel that something extraordinary was about to happen. On his fifth attempt the Special Olympian raised his right leg and balanced on his left leg for approximately five seconds. For a healthy person this might not seem like much of an accomplishment, but we suggest that this is the same peak performance state that has led many physically-gifted Olympians to world records. The crowd in the gymnasium stood and cheered. Some openly cried. There was a feeling of awe for what had been witnessed. Make no mistake nothing is impossible!

The authentic performer is able to access an awareness-centered consciousness which has the ability to adapt to the physical task at hand. Human history is full of stories such as mothers gaining a sudden burst of adrenaline needed to give them the strength to pick up a car to save their child. The human body has abilities that, under ordinary consciousness, would be impossible. Awareness-centered consciousness has the ability to take the body beyond scientifically-accepted physical limits and literally alter the body's physical makeup.

Jacques Mayol

One such story is that of the legendary no-limits underwater free-diving champion, Jacques Mayol.

No-limits free-diving is a sport that uses weighted sleds to descend under water for as long as competitors can hold their breath. Air balloons then insure a speedy ascent to the surface when the air in their lungs runs out. Mayol had a passion for free diving based on his love for the ocean, his personal philosophy, and his desire to explore his own limits. His diving philosophy sought to reach a state of mind, through relaxation and yoga, whereby he could accomplish apnea. Apnea is the suspension of external breathing, where there is no movement of the muscles of respiration and the volume of air in the lungs remains unchanged. Mayol studied the breathing techniques of Dolphins and had developed a friendship with a dolphin in Miami named Clown. The two would frequently swim and dive under water together.

Between 1966 and 1983, Mayol was eight-time no-limits diving champion. In 1976 he broke the 100 meter barrier with a 101-meter dive off of the coast of Elba, Italy. Tests showed that as he began his descent under the surface of the water his heartbeat decreased from 60 to 27 beats per minute. This is an aspect of the respiration system known as the "mammalian diving reflex," a reflex that is more evident in whales, seals, and dolphins than humans. Awareness-centered consciousness can alter the body's chemistry, enabling it to reach a peak performance state that might not be thought possible.

Never underestimate the miraculous capacity of the body to adapt to physical challenges in awareness-centered consciousness. When the body experiences peak performance, it is time to sustain, perform, and live within that peak performance state — the state of enlightenment.   Let's discover the absolute cause for the evolution of life and sports. Welcome to the power of spirit!

Chapter 8
Spiritual: Pathway to Enlightenment

The spiritual pathway is your relationship to God. In sports, the spiritual pathway can either unify and sustain, or separate and deplete, the energy for peak performance. It all hinges on whether it is approached through awareness-centered consciousness or ego-centered consciousness.

Ego-Centered Consciousness on the Spiritual Pathway

In ego-centered consciousness on the spiritual pathway, the inherent duality of opposing forces deals with pride and humiliation. Even if you have accessed awareness-centered consciousness and played your sport "in the zone," the ego will want to take credit, control, and replicate any heightened performance and experience, that occurred as a result of clearing tension on the first six pathways.   We call this pathway the "ego's last stand" because the ego will tend to be threatened by its own loss of identity inherent in spiritual awareness.

Ego-centered consciousness on the spiritual pathway seeks to manifest itself as pride in the self. The ego desires to condition pride, which is the high end of the ego, and thus avoids the low end of the ego, which is humiliation. The act of either desiring pride or resisting humiliation programs a new cycle of separation and duality while re-introducing tension, sending the athlete spiraling back down into ego-centered consciousness on all the pathways. This is the ultimate last trick of the ego because the ego is an isolating force.

Ego-centered consciousness is always working toward separation on the spiritual pathway. The ego tries to separate you from God.

In sports, the ego separates the individual from God by taking personal credit for the athletic performance and not giving credit to a higher power.

Awareness-Centered Consciousness on the Spiritual Pathway

In awareness-centered consciousness, the act of humility or giving credit to God, or a source greater than oneself, neutralizes the desire and resistance of pride and humiliation. Awareness-centered consciousness recognizes that peak performance is a gift from God that cannot be controlled, replicated, or trained for. It is an out-of-mind experience, a sense of selfless action, which can only be experienced through what author Eckhart Tolle calls the "power of now," or what we refer to as the miracle of the moment.

In awareness-centered consciousness the mind, body, and spirit are a unified whole connected to source energy acting through you. There is no sense of an identity to be threatened for there is no separation between you and others, the world, or God. In awareness-centered consciousness on the spiritual pathway, serving others and God is primary. It exists beyond the duality of pride, humiliation or any other separation.
The spiritual pathway in awareness-centered consciousness expands

the feel of the other six pathways. It creates balance between the unknown and the known, the inner and the outer, and the formless and form. This balance is created because there is no personal ego-credit for performance. There is a surrendering of the "I" and an offering of glory to God. Many might say that God has no place in sports. Players who cross themselves or point to the sky are often ridiculed by other players and the media. This topic has been brought to the forefront on a national stage by Heisman-winning quarterback and winner of two national championships at the University of Florida, Tim Tebow.

Tim Tebow

Tebow, coming out of college, was considered by NFL draft experts to be a third or fourth-round draft pick, at best. Given the speed of NFL defenses, his flawed, over-elongated throwing motion was considered a detriment to delivering the ball to the receivers.   His flawed throwing motion, combined with his inconsistent accuracy, made his NFL future as a quarterback questionable.

Josh McDaniels, a former Bill Belichick prodigy, took a chance on Tebow with a first round pick, 25th overall in the 2010 NFL draft. McDaniels saw many intangibles in Tebow, including leadership, great character, and off-the-charts competitiveness, which went behind his obvious athleticism. McDaniels considered him to be the type of player who would make everyone around him better.

In 2011, the Denver Broncos fired Josh McDaniel and hired John Fox as their head coach. Broncos legend, John Elway, was named their general manager. It appeared that the duo was looking for a more traditional quarterback who could stand in the pocket and throw the ball accurately. When the broncos got off to a one and four start, however, Tim Tebow was given a chance to start. He was able to win seven of the next eleven games, which was good enough to win the AFC west. The real miracle was not in winning when the experts said it could not be done, but rather that out of the seven games, Tebow engineered six fourth-quarter comebacks or overtime victories. This was the most in NFL history in that span of time and the odds of engineering all these comebacks is a staggering 300,000 to 1.

Tebow became known for kneeling down on one knee after a touchdown or the end of a game and giving glory to God. This became known as "Tebowing." His fourth quarter comebacks seemed to fall more under the category of divine inspiration than of luck or chance. Through his consciousness, he was able to elevate his play as well as that of others around him. We are not maintaining that God was somehow on his side and against his opponents, but rather that higher consciousness on the spiritual pathway can lift sports performance to miraculous heights.

The Ego Performer on the Spiritual Pathway

The ego performer on the spiritual pathway experiences a state somewhere between pride and humiliation. Pride is often thought to be a desired attribute in our society. Coaches want their teams to take pride in their performance. Pride in the tradition of a team has been shown to be a strong component of success.   It can be seen at every level of competition and is probably the single greatest motivational force of the ego. It is very evident in tradition-rich football schools such as Miami, Michigan, Oklahoma, Alabama, Florida, USC, Notre Dame, and Ohio State, to name just a few. Basketball teams such as Kentucky, Kansas, Indiana, Duke, and North Carolina give rise to great pride. Creating greater pride in tradition is a major recruiting tool that all schools strive for. It attracts both potential athletes and money.   It is no coincidence that teams with the most pride and tradition tend to get the better players. Pride, however, can quickly turn into spiritual quicksand because what goes up will often come down. When things start to go bad there seems no way out.

Motivating through the fear of humiliation is a common tool of many coaches. Techniques such as punishing the group for one person's failure, calling out players in front of peers, degrading comments and pulling players out of practice and games are designed to keep players motivated. The military uses humiliation as a way of training soldiers who will obey commands and die for their country. The philosophy by which they develop soldiers is to first break down individual pride, partly by using humiliation, and then to build them up with a sense of pride in a group identity — "You are now a marine!"

Bobby Knight

Bobby Knight, the famous basketball coach known as "The General," probably employed military humiliation techniques to motivate and teach his players. One of Knight's first coaching jobs was at West Point Military Academy, where Knight "whipped" his players to fit the style of offense and defense that he valued. He was an innovating coach, employing a motion offense, a system requiring complete cooperation and discipline from all of his players. It was probably "Knight's way or the highway."

Knight, regarded as one of the greatest coaches of all time, moved on to become the head coach of the Indiana Hoosiers, where he won three national championships and numerous Big-Ten titles. He also coached the U.S Olympic team to a gold medal in 1994. His pride was brought to the forefront in September of 2000, when he became upset when a 19 year old student addressed him by saying, "What's up, Knight?" It was alleged that Knight grabbed the student by the arm, and cursed at him for his lack of respect. Earlier that year, for other separate incidents, Knight was put under a no-tolerance mandate. It is likely that the school did not want to suffer any embarrassment or humiliation by any of Knight's antics or questionable behavior. He was told not to put Indiana University in a bad light.

Knight's behavior ultimately led to his dismissal. In a way, this was a great travesty because he worked very hard to turn kids into men and had a high rate of graduation from his players. But it seems as though the perception of pride and humiliation was the major factor at work in his being fired as head coach. The school's pride likely came into conflict with Knight's pride. The school's pride won.

Many great coaches try to condition an association between pride in winning and humiliation in losing. The stronger the feelings associated with pride in winning and humiliation in losing that an athlete has, the more motivated they are, because fear of being humiliated is an extremely strong motivational force. Societies are, to a great extent, conditioned to admire winners and scorn losers. Fans carry this conditioning along also to sporting events. They associate with the feeling of pride if their team wins or humiliation if their team loses. Some professional football teams have gone on losing streaks only to see their fans attend games wearing bags over their heads out of embarrassment to be associated with the team. Stories abound around the world of fights breaking out at soccer games. In some instances people have been killed by rioting fans. These fights are rooted and fueled by the motivation of pride and humiliation.

The Miami Dolphins

Pride in accomplishment can have an effect on a team or individual throughout a lifetime. Such is the case with many members of the 1972 Miami Dolphins, who are the only team to go through an entire season without losing a game. Since that 1972 team, whenever a team gets close to going undefeated it invokes a discussion about which is the greatest of all time. It is documented Some players from the Miami Dolphins Super Bowl team from 1972, such as Bob Kuechenberg, Mercury Morris, Nick Buoniconti, Dick Anderson, Larry Little and Paul Warfield, phone each other yearly to reminiscence about that perfect 1972 season. In addition, members of the team will get together to celebrate a champagne toast to the first loss to the last undefeated team of that season. They have made many such toasts because there has never been another undefeated team since. This display of pride has caused many fans, players, coaches, and commentators from other teams to resent them and want to belittle their accomplishment. Their feeling is that if you can knock someone down a peg by belittling their accomplishment, you can take away some of their pride. It really comes down to a battle for pride. "If you take all the pride, there is none left for me." There is a battle in sports and society in general over who deserves the most pride. The insatiable desire to feel pride and the resistance to humiliation is at the root of most conflicts and is a destructive influence in the world.

The Authentic Performer on the Spiritual Pathway

The authentic performer on the spiritual pathway transcends the duality of pride and humiliation, feeling instead a sense of grace, compassion, and humility. They realize that they are a blessed and fortunate receiver of God-given talents and opportunities. The authentic performer understands that surrendering their pride or ego enhances the quality of their sports performance and every aspect of life. They realize that pride blocks feel and can only take them so far in sports performance. Ultimately, spiritual divine inspiration is the greatest motivation, greater than any amount of pride that is conditioned through the ego.

The authentic performer always gives care and attention to the process of the sporting event. Rather than trying to attain personal glory and personal achievement, they are immersed in the process of raising the collective consciousness. In return for raising the collective consciousness, they experience a greater feel for the process and a higher level of performance.

The authentic performer is in a spiritual state connected to God and source energy. The creative process itself flows through the authentic performer. They create their performance from God as the center, realizing that consciousness itself is the only cause. Everything else is effect.

Andrea Jaeger

Sometimes the conditioning of the ego performer to have great pride as motivation to reach the pinnacle of their sport can be surrendered, moving a player towards a spiritual life. One such story is the remarkable story of Andrea Jaeger.

Jaeger was a childhood tennis prodigy with stardom written all over her game. She was considered by many the best player of her generation, turning pro at the tender age of 14 in 1981. Even at the age of 13 she was capable of competing with and beating professional players. Trained by her father, an ex-boxer known for his strict discipline style, it was alleged that she was often punished with physical and mental abuse when she did not follow his training and advice.

Although she had excelled at tennis at a very young age, she always felt the need to help others. She often struggled on the tennis court because it seemed as though she could not rectify ego gratification and selflessness with a more spiritual path. She could not find a way to mesh spirituality and service to others with competitive sports. Even with this internal conflict she was ranked number two in the world in 1983. Just like an animal trapped in a cage, however, she constantly looked for a way out.

Andrea Jaeger was referred to by other players and the media as "the brat," but we feel in reality that her "acting out" was a reflection of her ego suffering and the pain she felt from putting fame and fortune over heart, sacrifice and service to others. Likely she never felt comfortable in her own tennis skin. As strange as it would seem to most, Jaeger admitted that she did not always feel good about beating her opponents. In 1984, Jaeger suffered a shoulder injury. She saw this as a blessing in disguise rather than a curse. In 1987, after only 6 years on the tour, she retired. She took her tour winnings, some 1.4 million dollars, and started "The Little Star" foundation to help terminally ill children.

It was clear that her talent as a tennis player was in opposition to her calling. She followed her heart and decided to serve God rather than serve her ego. In 2006, she continued on her spiritual path and became a nun. She said that she had never been happier in her life. Authentic Sports is not suggesting that sports and a spiritual path are not compatible. Instead, we offer a way to play sports at the highest level through evolving consciousness. Contrary to traditional opinion, peak performance is a spiritual state.

Bethany Hamilton

The next story illustrates how sports and spirituality are, in fact, unified. Rarely does an athlete suffer an apparent career-ending, traumatic injury and then move back to the top of their sport. But such is the case with the well-known surfer, Bethany Hamilton, who became known as the soul surfer. This was a term coined in the 1960`s, used to describe one who surfs for the pure joy and pleasure of surfing. On October 31, 2003, at the age of 13, Bethany was attacked by a 13 foot tiger shark at Tunnels Beach in Kauai, Hawaii. Her left arm was ripped off just below the shoulder. Fortunately, the father of her best friend, with whom she was surfing, saved her life by fashioning a tourniquet that kept her from bleeding to death. She was rushed to the hospital. By the time she got there she had lost sixty percent of her blood.

Watching movies such as *Jaws* have kept people out of the ocean by creating great fear of shark attacks. One can only imagine actually living through such a terrifying experience. But less than one month after this horrific incident Bethany got back on her board and started surfing again. Her dream of becoming a professional surfer was not going to be derailed by the shark attack.

She and her families' great faith helped give Bethany the courage to return to the ocean. In 2004, she won best-comeback of an athlete on the ESPYS awards. She continued her amazing dream, finishing second in her first professional competition. But this is much, much more than a story of personal triumph. Bethany`s story became an inspiration not just for sports competitors but for anyone disabled. She raised the bar to show what is possible for others despite any apparent adversity. She is quoted as saying, "this has been a special

126

life that I could not have planned on my own." In an interview she was asked if she would change anything, given the opportunity. Her answer was an unequivocal no. She felt that the shark attack enabled her to be of greater inspiration and service to more people. She would sacrifice her arm to help others. This sense of sacrificing to be a blessing for others is the pinnacle of the spiritual pathway.

When sacrificing, as a blessing for others, occurs in the middle of a competition it is an extraordinary and consciousness transforming event. The ego's desire to feel pride and to win at all costs overshadows spiritual qualities such as sacrifice, compassion, and selfless action. When a story takes place that contains these higher conscious qualities, the consciousness of every human being is uplifted.

Tucholosky / Holtman

In a Division III softball game between Central Washington and Western Oregon, with an NCAA berth possibly on the line, Sara Tucholosky came up to the plate to bat. She was a part time outfielder for Western Oregon, and had only three hits in 34 at bats. Sara was not expected to play a major role in the game, but destiny knows no limits. With two teammates on base, Sara hit an unlikely home run over the center field fence. As she took the customary jog around the bases, she noticed that she had not touched first base. As she turned to go back to tag first base, she tore ligaments in her knee and fell to the ground. The rules stated that nobody on Sara's team could touch her and thereby help her around the bases, as it would result in an out. The only option that Sara`s coach had was to take the home run away from her and put a pinch runner on first. The Umpire would then record it as a two-run single. What would normally be the highlight of any athlete's college career, hitting a home run in the biggest game of the season, would now result in a single, adding insult to injury.

The first base coach for Western Oregon prepared to put in a pinch runner for Sara when she heard "excuse me, would it be okay if we carried her around the bases and she touched each base?" The voice belonged to Holtman, the star player for the opposing team Central Washington. Holtman, at the time, held almost every record in Central Washington history. Nothing in the college softball rule book stated that opposing team players could not help an injured player around the bases.

Holtman, who had also suffered from knee injuries in her career, was probably overwhelmed by compassion which neutralized her ego. This allowed her to be in a higher state of consciousness, creating the space for a selfless action. Neither team had ever been to the NCAA tournament in school history, so this selfless act could cost Central Washington the game. Holtman and the shortstop lifted Sara and carried her around the bases, allowing Sara to touch each base. As she was carried around the infield there was a sense of joy in the stadium, as the fans in the grandstand gave them a standing ovation.

As it so happened, this selfless act may have cost Central Washington the game. They lost to Western Oregon, 4 runs to 2. Coach Knox of Western Oregon said that this selfless act of service, demonstrated by Holtman and her teammate, changed her personally. Spirit transforms and uplifts consciousness, having an effect on all humankind.

Chapter 9
Surrendering the Ego: Preparing
Consciousness for Peak Performance

By now we hope we have made our point that peak performance will never be the outcome of ego-centered consciousness. The good news is that the ego is not who you really are. It is a conditioned program that has stolen your true identity, the authentic self. The ego reverse engineers reality, convincing you that what are really effects are instead causal. For example, you watch a sporting event and notice one team dominating another team. Rather than realizing that it is the process which creates the result, the ego sees domination as the cause and the key to winning. This addiction to the result causes the ego to always work backwards *from* the result, which disconnects process and feel from the present moment. Process and feel in the present moment are the hallmarks of peak performance.

While it is tempting for us to offer some type of "technique," a step-by-step "how-to" that will guarantee your success, our experience tells us that doing so would be treading on dangerous ground because the ego loves techniques, anything that it can try to grab onto as the "answer." Soon the technique becomes the object of the ego's worship, the thing that is going to "save" the ego from itself.

But bringing such a mindset into using a technique quickly renders the technique ineffective. The technique may be designed to get you out of the ego, but if your ego is trying to get something out of the technique, then you are stuck in the very mindset that is causing you problems in the first place. The ego is relentless!

So offering practical advice in this area is a very tricky business. Rather than giving any specific technique, our approach is to offer guiding principles. Our intention is for you to take these principles, expand them through awareness (observation mode), and enhance your own personal feel. Everyone is different. Use these principles in accordance with individual personal feel or the principles that resonate within. While these principles and the following meditation are centered on sports performance they will elevate any activity in human experience.

Guiding Principles for Preparing Consciousness for Peak Performance

1. Realizing that the ego and your thoughts are not you is essential for peak performance. You *have* thoughts but you are *not* your thoughts. If you are not aware of the ego's intent to keep you a prisoner of the thought program, you will revert back to ego-centered consciousness.

2. Clearing tension in the body, mind, and spirit through breathing and a mindfulness check will allow you to access awareness-centered consciousness. Mindfulness is a passive state which allows you to observe and feel energy blocks or restricted feel in your body, mind, and emotions. As you surrender the ego, your natural feel state or authentic self will awaken.

3. Neutralizing the tension on each pathway allows you to go deeper and expand feel, unblocking deeper layers of tension that go unnoticed. Like a washing machine that is on but not registered on your senses until someone turns it off, there are deeper layers of tension that are engrained into your mental, emotional, reactive pattern. These patterns are hidden and not noticeable for the most part until the tension is brought to your attention.

The *Seven Pathways* will guide you toward becoming aware of and releasing hidden layers of blocked energy and restricted feel. Each pathway is based in duality and opposing forces which divide attention. Like a pendulum, the mind oscillates between these two opposites. If you can feel or sense these opposing forces, it neutralizes the ego on that pathway.

The tension on each pathway comes to light when attention is given to sports performance. An athlete putting attention on the pathway in relationship to the performance of their sport will stir up hidden levels of tension in the body, mind, and emotions. This tension is ultimately based in the desire for the high end of the ego while resisting the low end of the ego. Each pathway has its own opposing opposite which is desired and resisted by the ego.

As we have said before, you cannot have the positive or desired side without the resisting or negative side when it comes to the ego. The desired side feels more like a pulling or attracting force and the resisted side feels more like a pushing or repelling force. This tug of war, the feeling of opposing forces pushing and pulling, exists on each pathway.

131

**Guided meditations for releasing energy blocks
and the resulting restricted feel on the Seven Pathways**

1. **Will Pathway**: With attention on your sporting event and your sports performance, notice your level of desire to win as well as your resistance to losing. Become aware of how strong your will or desire is for success while observing your resistance to failure. Notice any tension that arises as a result of putting your attention on the will pathway. The mere observation alone will dissipate blocked energy and expand feel. It may seem counter-intuitive and paradoxical, but realizing that by surrendering both your ego's desire to win and resistance to losing will lead to a higher or greater will.

2. **Belief Pathway**: With attention on your sporting event and your sports performance, notice your level of desire for "I can," or confidence, as well as your resistance to "I can't," or doubt. Be aware of how strong your desire for self-belief is. Note also any resistance to self-doubt that you have. Notice any tension that arises as a result of putting your attention on the belief pathway. Observation, as it removes tension, will dissipate blocked energy and expand feel. Releasing or surrendering the limitation of beliefs leads to an extraordinary performance.

3. **Mental Pathway**: With attention on your sporting event and your sports performance, notice your desire and level of attachment to certain subjective experiences that you judge as being good, and your resistance to other subjective experiences that you judge as being bad. Be aware of how strong your attachment to your desire for good experiences is. But note as well your repelling and resistance to bad experiences. Notice any tension that arises from putting your attention on the mental pathway. Observation, as it removes tension, will dissipate blocked energy and expand feel. By releasing or surrendering all attachments to the judgments of good

and bad in relation to your performance leads to an empty mind state, allowing your energy to be focused in the present.

4. **Emotional Pathway**: With attention on your sporting event and your sports performance, notice your level of desire for positive emotions or feelings, and your resistance to negative emotions and feelings. Be aware of the strength of your desire to express and feel positive emotions. Notice as well how much you want to suppress negative emotions. Note any tension that arises from putting your attention on the emotional pathway. Observation, as it removes tension, will dissipate blocked energy and expand feel. By releasing and surrendering all your desire for positive emotion as well your resistance to negative emotion will lead to an effortless flow of energy.

5. **Relationship Pathway**: With attention on your sporting event and sports performance, notice your level of desire for yourself or team as well as your resistance against the other player or team. Be aware of the strength of your desire to overcome your opponent. Also be aware of your resistance to being overcome by your opponent. Notice any tension that arises from putting your attention on the relationship pathway. Observation, as it removes tension, will unblock energy and expand feel. By releasing and surrendering all desire for separation between you and your opponent, more energy will be available.

6. **Physical Pathway**: With attention on your sporting event and sports performance, notice your level of desire for physical strength and your resistance to physical weakness. Be aware of how strong your desire is to physically control the body and physically dominate the conditions of contest while resisting physical weakness and submitting to the conditions of contest. Notice any tension that arises from putting your attention on the physical pathway.

Observation, as it removes tension, will unblock energy and expand feel. By releasing and surrendering all desire for physical strength while resisting physical weakness, energy becomes relaxed and centered in the body.

7. **Spiritual Pathway**: With attention on your sports event and sports performance, notice your level of desire to be prideful in the self. Note, too, your resistance to feeling or experiencing humiliation. Be aware of the strength of your desire to possess and take credit for your performance. Observe how strong your resistance is to defeat and criticism. Notice any tension that arises from putting attention on the spiritual pathway. Observation, as it removes tension, will unblock energy and expand feel. By releasing and surrendering all desire for pride and resistance to humiliation, energy will be transformed into a pure state of being.

Now that you have surrendered your ego on each of the Seven Pathways, you are ready to prepare your consciousness for peak performance. Without question, what you prepare in consciousness will show up in form or action. Now that you have made the shift into awareness-centered consciousness you can plant the seeds for peak performance on each pathway.

1. **Will Pathway**: With attention on your sporting event, connect to core intentions such as "mastery of the game." Allow your natural intrinsic motivation to awaken. Create the "feel" impression that the process of playing the sport itself inspires you.

2. **Belief Pathway**: With attention on your sporting event or sports performance, embrace the unknown. Allow a sense of faith that will move you past all limitations. Create the feel impression that you are in the realm of all possibilities.

134

3. **Mental Pathway**: With attention on your sporting event or sports performance, embrace a sense of acceptance and detachment from all judgment. Create a feel impression of your mind being free, intuitive, and receptive.

4. **Emotional Pathway**: With attention on your sporting event or sports performance, embrace a sense of appreciation. Create the feel impression of your emotions flowing freely and feeling a sense of joy.

5. **Relationship Pathway**: With attention on your sporting event and sports performance, embrace your connection to your opponent and others. Create the feel impression of compassion, a sense that "we're all in this together," and the feeling of unity.

6. **Physical Pathway**: With attention on your sporting event and sports performance, embrace the body's wisdom. Create the feel impression of a rhythm with the environment and a sense of effortless effort.   —   .

7. **The Spiritual Pathway**: With attention on your sporting event and sports performance, embrace a sense of humility. Recognize that this is a gift from God. Create the feel impression that the performance is coming through you, that you are a receiver of it and that you experience the feeling of an enlightened state.

Do not underestimate the power in the shift from ego-centered consciousness into awareness-centered consciousness. The power in this process will change the quality of your consciousness and transform your athletic performance and life. Each time you surrender your ego and prepare your consciousness through awareness, it will have a profound effect on any performance in the future..

Chapter 10
Beyond Authentic Sports: The Peak Performance Life

The quality of your consciousness equals both the quality of your sports performance and the quality of your life. The world of sports is a microcosm of a bigger world view that can be lived either through ego-centered consciousness or awareness-centered consciousness. Unfortunately, human history often reflects a story of life being dominated by ego-entered consciousness. Living through ego-centered consciousness will always result in drama, conflict, and struggle. If the ultimate mission for humankind is cooperation, peace and harmony on earth, then the ego, with its personal agenda, is not the solution. Fortunately, there have been glimpses of awareness-centered consciousness throughout our history. One can find many stories wherein people's actions and deeds reflect a higher state of consciousness.

Authentic Sports recognizes that the ego has served as a necessary aspect of human consciousness throughout human history as a vehicle for survival. Our deepest hope and wish is to make the ego the secondary player in life on earth and to make awareness-centered consciousness, or the authentic self, the primary player.

What shows up in the world of action and form, when the ego is the primary player in life? As we have said, the ego is who you think you are. So the ego has many strategies to protect its identity. They include, but are not limited to, safety, permanence, personal power, and security. The ego is continuously and relentlessly concerned with its own actualization and the pursuit of "more." It's thought program involves comparison, judgment, ranking, measuring, blaming, manipulating, complaining, labeling and rationalizing. These are but a few of the ego's tools that it uses to manufacture its ultimate goal, the total sense of separation. The ego is an isolating force and its accompanying separative movement of thought is the source of all conflict, drama, and struggle in the world.

When the ego is the primary player in life, the seven pathways become the playing field for opposition and destruction.

1. When the ego on the will pathway becomes the primary player in life the will becomes engaged in a battle against other "wills" or forces. These opposing forces are very evident in political systems (Republican vs. Democrat), religions (Christianity vs. Muslim), ideologies (Democracy vs. Communism), and relationships (husband vs. wife).

2. When the ego on the belief pathway becomes the primary player in life, beliefs are seen as absolute truth that must be followed at all cost. Beliefs, on the ego pathway, divide and separate races, religions, countries and personal relationships. These divisions have led to many human atrocities including genocide, slavery, religious crusades, holy wars, terrorism and world wars.

3. When the ego on the mental pathway becomes the primary player in life, the mind operates from a programmed past and force of habit. It becomes a slave to its program. Thinking serves the ego's destructive habits. The mind perpetuates human suffering

based on its desire and resistance program.

4. When the ego on the emotional pathway becomes the primary player in life's emotions, it becomes dependent upon getting what it wants and identifying with separation. Positive emotions are a reaction to getting what you want and negative emotions are a reaction to not getting what you want. Emotions and feeling reactions such as revenge and jealousy have led to many stories of misery and human suffering.

5. When the ego on the relationship pathway becomes the primary player in life, others become a threat. The ego desires to see itself, country, religion and beliefs as better than, more deserving than, smarter than or morally superior to others. It seeks to dominate and conquer any perceived threat. There is a constant tension between "for and against" that leads to confrontation in all areas of life.

6. When the ego on the physical pathway becomes the primary player in life it leads to physical abuse to both the human body and nature. Disease, pollution, global warming, endangered species and the deterioration of the rain forests are but a few of the destructive effects of the ego on the physical pathway.

7. When the ego on the spiritual pathway becomes the primary player in life, pride becomes the foundation of human existence — pride in self, accomplishment, job, title, deeds, money, country, family, gangs, community, team, church, religion, philosophy and ideology becomes the cornerstone for all relationships. Pride is at the heart of most, if not all conflict and suffering in the world. It is the ego's last stand and the ultimate separation between us and God or source.

What shows up in the world of actions and form when the authentic self is the primary player in life? The authentic self creates through awareness-centered consciousness. This is who you really are. You are pure consciousness, beyond the known and all past programming. The authentic self is nonjudgmental and does not have a personal agenda. It is connected to source energy (God). When the authentic self is the primary player in life, all actions, and deeds, work towards the best interest of the whole.

The authentic self has no resistance to what is. You are a receiver of God's intention. You are not motivated by the secret agendas of the ego such as pleasure and permanence. You are connected to the creative process itself. When the authentic self is the primary player in life, the seven pathways become a playing field for expanding consciousness and creating a better world.

1. When the authentic self on the will pathway is the primary player in life, personal will becomes aligned to divine will. Divine will unites people based on similarities and a higher purpose. Authentic will moves politics, religion, ideologies and relationships toward common ground and a core intention centered in peace and tolerance.

2. When the authentic self on the belief pathway is the primary player in life, beliefs are seen simply as a viewpoint through which we experience reality. The authentic self recognizes that beliefs that do not serve the world and the whole of humankind are not based in truth. The authentic self realizes that faith, transcending belief, is what allows humankind to experience the realm of all possibility. When the authentic self is the primary player in life, religion is based on spiritual principles, governments are based on integrity, justice, and equality, countries are based on peacefulness and harmonious coexistence, and relationships are based in honesty and cooperation.

3. When the authentic self on the mental pathway is the primary

player in life, the mind is in the present moment and thinking serves awareness and God. The authentic self's mind is free from the desire and resist program of judging everything through the filter of good and bad. The mind is not a slave to the ego or the survival of the self, so it is free to be inventive and creative in ways that improve the quality of life for everyone.

4. When the authentic self on the emotional pathway is the primary player in life, there is a sense of appreciation for whatever happens. Life is seen as a gift and all emotions are motivated by a feeling of giving joy and love to others. The authentic self on the emotional pathway feels compassion for everyone.

5. When the authentic self on the relationship pathway is the primary player in life, others are perceived as valued teachers. There is a sense of seeking together and creating a win-win situation. There is a feeling of responsibility for the well-being of others. Everyone is treated as having value and a God given talent which can benefit the whole.

6. When the authentic self on the physical pathway is the primary player in life, it leads to health, balance, a sense of well-being, clean air and water, and preservation of both land and life. All life and nature is embraced with care and attention. When you give care and attention to your body and environment, you experience the peak performance life.

7. When the authentic self on the spiritual pathway is the primary player in life, humility and sacrifice is the foundation for life. A sense of oneness or unity becomes the cornerstone of all relationships. There is the realization that every aspect of yourself and everything that you have is a blessing from God and that it is only through the gift of grace that enlightenment and peak performance are possible.

Throughout Authentic Sports we have used multiple athletes and their sports performances to illustrate the difference between ego-centered consciousness and awareness centered consciousness. Authentic Sports feels that an athlete's inner reality or level of consciousness in sports is a microcosm of the world as a whole. Higher consciousness is the source for both peak performance in sports and life. If you raise consciousness, you expand feel, and you put the peak in a peak performance life.

All through history you can find examples of people living through the ego mind with its separative movement of thought and its potential destructive nature. Memories of atrocities, violence, and death at the hands of people like Genghis Kahn, Hitler and Osama Bin Laden are etched in our minds. Fortunately, enlightened beings living in awareness centered consciousness have neutralized negative energy through the unified movement of thought. Spiritual figures such as Jesus, the Buddha, Lao Tzu, and the mother Theresa, to name a few have brought the truth of spiritual consciousness to our planet. These spiritual figures embody higher principles such as love, grace, compassion, kindness and humility which are pathways to an enlightened society. They demonstrated that through the inner quality of consciousness or the integration of spirit and form the world will be transformed. The rising tide of consciousness will bring up all the ships. Authentic Sports offers a gentle wish or prayer that we may all work together, God centered, to transform the world into an enlightened state.

Acknowledgements

Special acknowledgement goes to Bruce Donaldson for his insights and immeasurable contributions to Authentic Sports.

Special thanks to Gayle Lefko for her hours of patience, detailed work, articulation and gift of clarity.

Special thanks to Courtney Lefko for his gift of enthusiasm, constant support and helping to optimize the energy of the book.

Special thanks to Lorrie Moneymaker for her unconditional support, patience and understanding.

Special thanks Clifford Burns for his creative insights and his gift of seeing outside the box.

Special thanks to Marc Maxwell who believed in us to get us started.

Special thanks to Jim Willis for his belief that inspired books need to get out into the world.

Thanks to the following people for their encouragement: Kellie Lefko, Bobby Conover, Randall Meade, Oletha Meade, Scott Okarski and all family members, supporters and students.

About the Authors

Bill Lefko is a professional tennis coach with over 40 years and 40,000 hours of on-court teaching experience. He has a background in Transcendental Meditation, Neuro-linguistics programming and a Philosophy/Psychology major at Austin Peay State University in Clarksville, Tennessee. He has spent his lifetime studying teaching styles and systems in the game of tennis. He is the originator and co-author of Authentic Tennis, a holistic approach to learning tennis through the integration of spirit and swing. Bill Lefko currently resides in Hopkinsville, Kentucky with his wife Gayle and is involved in coaching tennis, writing, and raising consciousness.

Daniel Baird is a professional tennis instructor who has taught tennis for the last 28 years, primarily in the Daytona Beach, Florida area. He has taught over 18,000 hours of tennis to a broad range of students. He has taken a wide variety of courses over the last 25 years in the field of human consciousness and has integrated it into his tennis coaching. Daniel Baird is the co-author of Authentic Tennis with Bill Lefko and is the author of The Undiscovered Universe-The Revelation of the Creation. Daniel Baird currently lives in Ocala, Florida with his wife, Lorrie Baird.

Made in the USA
Columbia, SC
15 October 2018